My Spiritual Diary

My Spiritual Diary

DALE EVANS ROGERS

FLEMING H. REVELL COMPANY

Printed in the United States of America

Fourth Printing, April 1956

LIBRARY OF CONGRESS CATALOG NUMBER 55-5390

Westwood, N. J.—316 Third Avenue
Los Angeles 41—2173 Colorado Boulevard
London E.C.4—29 Ludgate Hill
Glasgow C.2—229 Bothwell Street

My Spiritual Diary

I am resolved to keep a spiritual accounting, that I may check on my soul's progression or (may God forbid!) regression.

So I set down here my faith, hope, philosophy and spiritual adventuring, that I may know how weak and strong I am.

Put Your hand over mine, Lord God, that this writing may be honest and reverent.

D. E. R.

Monday

TODAY we were very busy. Roy and I had to "tape" two commercial radio shows, and while we were in the NBC studios, Art Rush, our manager, gave us a wire from Sallie and Nadine Woods, of the Muscular Dystrophy Research Foundation, asking us to join their Prayer Crusade for the work they are doing.

Of course we were glad to help—but it was such short notice!

Roy asked me to help him write a prayer he could record, to be played on radio all over the state of Texas. I sat still for a moment and asked for divine guidance, and it came: our Lord suggested to me that we use the 12th, 13th and 14th verses of the 14th of John.

It flowed so easily then, into the prayer. And the words matched the occasion so much better than any poor human words could have matched it: "He that believeth on me, the works that I do shall he do also; and greater works than these shall he do, because I go unto my Father; And whatsoever ye shall ask in my name, that will I do, that the Father may be glorified in the Son."

As the recording needle pressed Roy's prayer into the wax, I prayed that God would speak through him in the spirit of the living Christ. I believe He did, for Roy's voice seemed suddenly to take on a vital, glowing authority that bespoke the grace of our Lord.

"Ask, and ye shall receive!" Why do we not ask more often, instead of trying to rely on our poor human powers? He has words waiting for our lips, work for our hands to do, full rich lives to be lived in His service.

Take my life, Oh God, and let it be rich and beautiful for Thee.

Tuesday

I'VE been thinking of another aspect of what happened at the studio yesterday. As I sat there listening to Roy's prayer, I silently committed to the Lord all those suffering with infirmities. And I couldn't help thinking of how closely sin is related to infirmity, suffering and death.

Jesus said to the palsied man, "Son, thy sins be forgiven thee; take up thy bed and walk." The Master must have known that the man had to be freed of his sin and guilt before the Healing Spirit could really take hold of his sick physical body.

When we have a fresh, open abrasion, we first cleanse the wound with an antiseptic, and then we apply the healing agent.

Could it be that when an innocent child like our precious Robin is afflicted, God ministers through her to those surrounding her, convicting them of sin and helplessness, and so turning them to the love and saving power of the Christ? Once I just wondered about that; now I am certain of it.

I thank you, Father, for sending me a Mongoloid child, because now I can truly appreciate the cross of Jesus Christ.

Wednesday

UNTIL we really suffer, we can never feel the beat of the heart of Christ.

Perhaps it isn't that way with everyone, at least in their minds. God brings us to Himself over many different roads. For my part, I traveled the road of pain. I never knew my Saviour until I came to my life's deepest pit.

He gave me a little blonde angel and I almost worshiped her—in a frightening intensity, maybe because of her helplessness. She was so pure, so angelic, so defenseless.

Then in His wisdom He took her. My heart cracked—but thank God He was there to glue it together again!

You see, when she was gone, *I turned in the direction whence she had gone.* I turned toward the bosom of the Great Shepherd. Since she would be in His arms,

I turned to look at Him, and I came to love and trust Him completely, for all the rest of my earthly life.

Tears are sent to wash our eyes and make sight of Him clearer. That I believe, now. Beyond that, I believe it is good for my soul to know that one day He shall wipe away all tears from our eyes, "and there shall be no more death, neither sorrow, nor crying, neither shall there be any more pain. . . ."

Until then, dear God, use my tears and suffering to cleanse me for Thy Kingdom and to bring others to its gates.

Friday

TODAY I have been thinking of Tom, my blessed son. God used Tom to bring me back into the fold of Christ, even before little Robin came. How all-wise, how merciful, is God!

He sent Tom, I know, to "prepare the way" for Robin . . . sent him to lead me back into a knowledge of the love of God and to enjoy the delights of heavenly grace and peace.

I was starving, spiritually, and if I had gone on starving I would have been too weak to stand up under the blow of Robin's death.

God saw that coming! He sent Tom to strengthen me so that I could stand the testing.

This, to me, is proof that He cared what happened to me. How blind we are to His ways, all through life! How can we be so insensitive to the touch of His hand on our arms, guiding us and holding us up—until we stumble over some great tragedy or sin, and almost fall! Then we sense that He catches us, and holds us. . . .

May I come to know You so well, my Father, that I shall never again be unaware of the strength and lift of the everlasting arms.

Saturday

TODAY, I didn't get to read my morning and evening Bible lessons—and I missed them more than I would have missed eating. But I did pray, and turn my thought to the Lord during the day. I suppose keeping exact routines in the Christian life is not so important as keeping our minds tuned in on His.

We were on location at the Iverson Ranch, and I got a wonderful surprise when, at two o'clock, the assistant director said I could go home! Took my mother shopping in the valley, and then we joined Roy at six, and went to the Eilers ranch, where we celebrated their 27th wedding anniversary. What a blessed experience it was to be in their home! The Spirit is felt there, definitely; and no one can visit there without feeling that Presence. If we only had more homes like that. . . .

After a wonderful buffet supper, our good friend Tim Spencer dedicated the song he had just written—"I Thank My Maker for Making Thee Mine,"—to Frances and Leonard Eilers. Their lovely daughter, Joy Eilers, accompanied him as he sang. It was the high spot of a heart-warming evening, with so many of our old friends present. Roy thanked God for blessing the Eilers home and what it stood for.

It stands for Christ. This is a home completely dedicated to the Master; everyone in it knows Christ, and follows Him. Frances Eilers knew my son Tom before she knew me, and she had been praying along with Tom for my surrender to the claims of Christ, for several years. What a blessing she has been to me! What a blessing are Christian friends, always!

And what a blessing is the fellowship we enjoy with these friends, in Christ. I think the Kingdom of God would collapse without this thing called fellowship; it is the heart pumping out the blood of the gospel. Caught up in that fellowship, the petty trials and differences of our lives disappear. Jesus bridges instantly any gaps of personal difference, when the parties concerned are committed Christians.

Don't ever let me get so busy, Lord, that I forget to hold out the right hand of fellowship —to those I know and love, and to those I ought to know and love.

Sunday

It is early Sunday morning, and the beauty of God is over all the face of the earth; it is so lovely that it hurts the heart. This is the day *He* hath made!

I have just finished reading a chapter in Eugenia Price's book, *Discoveries;* it is a book about her personal contacts with the Saviour. She insists that it is impossible for her to go anywhere, now, without knowing that He is at her side. How right she is! Jesus said, "Lo, I am with you alway." That "alway" rears up in our minds as big as a house. Don't let me forget it, Father. Help me never to embark on any vessel of endeavor, or pleasure, or work in which I would be embarrassed to take You. Where You can't be with me is no place for me to go.

Now it is time for my Sunday evening prayer. I rest on your promise now, Father, that "So He giveth His beloved sleep." Please guard my subconscious mind tonight, for you know I am defenseless in my sleep. It seems that Satan takes a delight in camping on my shoulder during the night, for so often I find myself waking with a clouded misted mind. And, many times, with grieving thoughts about little Robin.

Each morning I have to grapple with him for a little before the Light breaks through and I realize that, endlessly, "Joy cometh in the morning."

Give now Thine angels charge over me, O God, and make me to know that when I awake, Thou wilt be there.

Monday

MILDRED BURNES, my fine hairdresser and my friend, is sitting here with me, doing some needlepoint for a chair, while I have been finishing my morning prayers and Bible lessons. My mother and I had breakfast together at home. She returned thanks for us all, to our Lord. What a joy it is to hear my mother pray! Since my father left us last April, it is a constant source of comfort to know that my mother is not alone. The Saviour is her constant companion—and what better could she have?

Thank You, Lord, for helping me fight off that temptation today. No one can tell me that "there is no Satan, no error," and get away with it. I keep meeting him "head on," in all sorts of temptations, and I doubt that I am peculiar in that. Haven't I read somewhere that even the saints find it necessary to keep up a sort of running fight with the devil? My own little temptation today may seem insignificant to anyone else, so I think I will mention it to no one but You. But it was there, and it packed more power than I care to admit. We are all tempted like that.

It seems that the closer I get to Christ, the harder

Satan tugs at me. It helps to remember Jesus saying "Be of good cheer; I have overcome the world!" I know that I, too, can overcome Satan through the strength of Jesus, my Redeemer. I don't have to depend on my puny self—and when I say "puny," it's an understatement.

> *O Lord of hosts, blessed is the man that trusteth in Thee.*

Tuesday

WE ARE out on location, where we have a photographer shooting a series of special color pictures for a magazine, and also some advertising agency people. Some of the folks in our crew get impatient with them, at times. I don't, for I know they are here to shoot some publicity pictures to be used in connection with the Exceptional Children's Benefit Show next week, at the Shrine Auditorium. Before I met Christ and before Robin came, I might have been impatient with them, but not today! Work on the set, now, seems to get in the way of the work I want to do for these mentally retarded children all over the world. These little angels unaware are close to my heart. 'Way down inside me, I can hear little Robin's joyful laughter when the Lord opens a way for me to help those kids, in any way I can.

Sometimes, when I finish letters of Christian testimony to the desperate parents of afflicted children, I can see Robin's smile widen as I look up at her picture over my desk.

Hope I get home early enough this afternoon to churn some butter and have some fresh buttermilk for supper. And I want to put up some chili from that coarse ground venison. It will taste mighty good in about a month!

Our Father, give me eyes to see the marks of Thy hand on the common things of life, and never let me stop pointing out those marks to others.

Wednesday

ART RUSH, our manager, is leaving for New York today; he will go to see Billy Graham in Detroit about the prospect of our appearing with Billy at the London Crusade for Christ, next Spring.

That will take some adjusting, for our schedule calls for us to be in a lot of other places than England. But what's a schedule, compared to witnessing in such a Crusade?

I refuse to worry about schedules. The Lord will handle it as He sees best, and I am content that He take care of it.

Guide me, God that I may learn to take no thought for the morrow in any selfish way, and that I may understand that sufficient unto the day is the evil thereof.

Thursday

RIGHT now, I'm looking at a wide expanse of trees and rocks on a hill in front of me. No two rocks, no two trees, are identical. What a mind has our Creator! Some cynic says, "Oh, this is all a *chemical* process; the elements of nature shape the rocks and the trees." Very well—*but who made the elements, and who so guides the use of the elements that no two trees or rocks are ever alike?*

The same thing goes for Jesus Christ. I hear the cynics say, "Oh, He was just a good man, a great prophet." Even if that were true, even if by the wildest stretch of my imagination I could convince myself that He was a myth, I would still have to explain His superhuman influence upon the lives of men, no two of whom have ever been alike! And I would still love the Words attributed to Him, and still see His principles as the hope of the world, and I would still attempt to pattern my life after His commandments.

The marvelous thing about Christianity is that as you struggle to know more about Jesus, the more you earnestly seek Him, *the more you come to know that*

He is the God He claimed to be, and nothing short of it. He said, "Him that cometh to me, I will in no wise cast out," and I know that works, for I have experienced it myself.

The sincere heart, seeking truth, will ultimately find its way to the foot of the cross, and find God in Christ at the foot of the cross. The Holy Spirit is ever near to help us find Him there, and to win us to Him there.

I stumble often, and lose my way, Oh God; Guide Thou my feet and my mind, and bring me at last unto Thy holy hill.

Friday

WHEN a man is so burdened with a heavy load that he cannot rise up and walk, there is, plainly, only one thing to be done. The load must be removed.

I look at people all around me and wonder how many of them know what really is the matter with them—how many understand the load of sin and guilt they have been carrying for years that has kept them down, spiritually. They are filled with doubt, suspicion, envy, fear and futility; they find joy in nothing, and they wonder what is wrong!

I could tell them what is wrong. I, personally, carried such a load of sin and guilt for twenty-five years.

I was a pretty sorry case, spiritually, when my son Tom asked me in church one night if all was well with my soul. I can vividly remember drawing myself up in indignant, shocked "surprise" that he would ask me such a question, and answering, "Why of course all is well with my soul. I'm all right. I accepted Christ when I was ten years old!" That should have settled it.

It settled nothing. Inside, my defenses were crumbling, and all my desperate efforts and words couldn't hide that. I saw tears in my son's eyes, and I knew that he was looking with the eyes of Christian understanding and compassion right down into my darkened soul.

I very nearly broke into tears, there in the church, but somehow I fought them back. At home, later, the dam broke, and in a flood of tears I saw that Christ had reached out through my beloved boy and redeemed a lost sheep. I called Tom and told him he was right, and that I would go to church the following Sunday, make my peace with Christ, take a public stand and unite with the church. I did just that. Thus was the burden slipped from my back; thus was I enabled to get up and walk again in a world so beautiful and full of joy that I could scarcely believe it!

In an instant, as I stood there in my bedroom facing myself in horror and throwing myself on His mercy, *everything* was changed; the world and my life were different from that moment on. The relief, the joy and the knowledge that He had set my feet on "higher ground" was the greatest experience of my whole life.

There has never been any question in my mind since that Sunday when I handed Him my soul. Oh, yes, there have been temptations to sin, worry, anxiety, shattered personal dreams, loss of loved ones—but all this was my weakness, not His. He has remained the strong high rock in the storm and stress, and never have I failed to find comfort and wisdom and strength in that Rock!

"Lo, I am with you alway, even unto the end of the world." Lord, my whole life rests on that, now.

Saturday

SOME misunderstanding soul, signing his letter "Anonymous," wrote me today, enclosing an article entitled "Don't Try to Play God." He signed his letter, in red ink, "From a Friend."

It happens often, to those of us in the public eye. We get used to it. I used to just laugh it off as the work of a crank, but now, Father, I find myself wishing that somehow You and I might do something about such misunderstanding. Forgive me for mentioning it to You, Father, but You know who and where "Anonymous" is. Could You possibly give him word that I am not trying to "play" anything, especially in a religious sense?

I am simply trying to be a channel, open for You to use. No one could possibly "play" at such serious business as that!

The article my unidentified friend sent me is typical of today's Godlessness. It asks the old question, cynically, "Am I my brother's keeper?" It infers that those who are dedicated to Christ and His purpose are fanatics, trying to impose their beliefs on a self-satisfied world. The person who sent it must need You, desperately.

Be merciful to him, Father; and be merciful to me, too, if my motives ever become un-Christian, or I am tempted to "play" or to deceive, in any department of my life.

Sunday

AS MUCH as it hurts me to face it, I must: early this morning, driving across Laurel Canyon and thinking over the years that are gone, I realized suddenly that there isn't one of God's Commandments that I haven't broken, in one way or another—either by act, thought, or the spoken word. That's a pretty terrible record. I wonder what my earthly father would have thought and done if I had deliberately set out to disobey every order he ever gave me? I got spanked, as a child, for disobeying only *a few;* I hate to think of the punishment I deserve from You.

How merciful You are, Father! How much You must love us! It is too much for me to understand, too much for my little mind to grasp. It is overwhelming for me just to think of how God gave Himself in His Son, to this wayward and perverse and unbelieving civilization, as the supreme sacrifice on His altar of love, to redeem our souls. We certainly don't deserve it.

I don't understand it, but I believe it!

I see things dimly now, Father—as through a glass, darkly; it strengthens my faith tremendously to know that one day I shall see clearly, face to face . . . .

Monday

THOSE stirring seven words leaped right out of the Sermon on the Mount, this morning, when I witnessed the sad spectacle of perfectly sincere Christians quarrelling over their theologies: "Judge not, that ye be not judged!" This business of criticizing and condemning each other by otherwise fine Christians, on the basis of doctrine and theology, goes into my heart like a knife. *Why* must we do that? We have shamefully split and divided His Church, arguing over many things which are non-essentials to salvation, while the great essentials of the Kingdom wait! His instructions to us to preach and save and baptize are so amazingly simple that I wonder why and how we have been able to manufacture such abysmal confusion and theological conflict.

Judge not! Oh, Lord, help me to cast out the beam

in my own eye before I set myself up as the judge of another's theology. Give me, I pray, such an insatiable desire for Thy knowledge and truth that I won't have time to judge others. *Help me to love more and judge less.* Give me the grace to step aside and let Thee do the judging! Give me understanding and compassion for those who are suffering and who are in need, spiritually.

Above all, Father, forgive me for ever judging anyone more harshly than I judge myself. I stand more in need of Your judgment and forgiveness than anyone I know!

Tuesday

OH, IF I could only make some unbelieving folks understand! They seem to think I have "gone pious" because You have taken out of me all desire for some of my old, so-called "pleasures"—that I have "set myself up to be holy." Father, if I could only make them see that Dale Evans has died, and that a willing slave to Christ has been born in her place! When I asked You to make me over, that's exactly what happened.

Why, Father, I never really saw a tree until I saw it through the eyes of faith. I never really heard the song of a bird in the meadow, never enjoyed the rain, the snow, the wind or a sunset!

In the old days I was always getting and never giving, and seldom knowing joy. Now I am finding a joy in life I never knew was there; now I live gloriously, through *giving.*

"I am come that they might have life, and that they might have it more abundantly" was certainly meant for me! He who was penniless in Galilee has made me rich beyond reckoning, and I know not how to thank Him, except by trying to pass on the gold of His spirit to others. Help me to do that, God.

Wednesday

THEY are calling me to do a scene, and I am writing this while Mildred, my hairdresser, is curling my hair. She is an understanding soul; she goes all-out to help me write this witness to Your saving power. Mildred watched me closely while You wrote *Angel Unaware* through my hands, and she said one day that she had never seen anyone write so fast. She couldn't get over it—the speed of my hands on the paper.

I told her that You were literally pushing my hand, and it seemed to me that I had little or nothing to do with it. *Angel* was Your book, not mine.

Isn't it so with all who write their witness, in whatever form? Harriet Beecher Stowe always insisted that God wrote *Uncle Tom's Cabin*; her hand was "God-driven." So it was with the authors of the Bible; their hands were driven by the same irresistible force. "Inspiration" is hardly the word for it. God just takes over everything.

Father, into Thy hands I commit mine.

Thursday

LAST night Tim Spencer called and asked me if I would accept the position of Vice-President in the Hollywood Christian Group. I am reluctant to do that, Father. I know how important the Group is, and what a witness it can be to the film industry of Hollywood. I would have to give real time to the leadership of such a group of people, and I just don't know where I'd get the time to fill the post adequately. I'm a little afraid of "spreading myself too thin" in Christian work, right now—of taking on so many different duties that I'll do none of them well. I wonder . . .

But Tim said, "God understands the pressure you're under. . . ." That settled it. If I take this new job, and commit the whole thing into your hands, You'll see me through—so I'll take it.

Satan had my ear, there, for a little; the old rascal knows what an influence radio, movies and television wield in the minds of young people all over the world, and I'm sure he'd like to break up *any* Christian group of people connected with those industries, or bend them to his will. He would like to "sift like wheat" the members of the Hollywood Christian Group. Don't let him do that, Father. We need this thing. Bless our meetings on Monday nights, won't You? Thou art our strength and our life; make us increasingly aware of that.

> *"Let thy beauty be upon us, Oh Lord; and establish the work of thy hands upon us . . ." and make us to know in the Hollywood Group that people everywhere are watching our hands, our faces, our hearts and our profession of faith in Thee. Make it faith so strong and good that it will not be questioned.*

Saturday

ROY and the others went duck-hunting this morning; Cheryl and I caught up on some much needed sleep. I was to give my personal testimony at a big religious meeting in Stockton. As Cheryl and I drove along from Sacramento to Stockton, I silently asked the Lord to reveal His will for my testimony, and to tell me what He wanted me to "emphasize." How silly we do become, over this "emphasizing"—as though it were all up to *us!*

Dr. Jack MacArthur and Rev. Jack Holcomb came up to our suite in the hotel, and we got down on our knees and asked God to take over the meeting. All of a sudden, I knew I had been wrong in worrying so about the "emphasizing," about the details of my little part in it, and especially in worrying so about any "special approach" to the folks in the audience. It was as though I heard Christ say, "*I'll* do the talking. You just get up there and tell them the truth about what I did for you, and don't spare the horses! A lot of those people have guilt complexes a mile long—accumulated over the years. You'd better level with them, quick, and let them know that I came and died to save sinners like you and them!"

I confess, Father, that when Cheryl and I walked out on the stage in that huge Civic Auditorium, my knees nearly buckled and let me down. When I saw that big house packed clear to the top row in the balcony, I suddenly realized that some souls here might be won or lost to Christ, depending on how successful I would be in beating back my ego and putting You out in front! There were many ministers of the gospel on that stage; I knew they would be watching and listening,—carefully, too.

Jack MacArthur introduced me. I breathed a prayer for You to go to work on that crowd as I stepped up to the microphone. I don't know how I ever spoke my first words, or any of the rest of the words. They weren't my words, at all; they were Yours, and how they came! They just seemed to pour out in a flood, like the proverbial "oil out of a jug." You unloosed my tongue. And they *came,* Father—they came down the aisle and gave themselves to Christ. What a fool I was to worry about how to "approach" them!

Help them to know quickly what I know now, Father: that he will be at perfect peace whose mind is stayed on Thee.

Sunday

How it does grieve me to see Christians back-slide because they refuse to come and take Your food regularly! By food I mean the Bible and communion with their fellow-Christians. They let their strength run low, and when they are weak and at their lowest point of resistance, Satan grabs them.

And he taunts them for years with a guilty conscience, and they are ashamed to face You, and just go on staying away from the Bible and from Christian fellowship. Sometimes it takes long, long years before they gain the courage to turn and face You once more and say, "All right, Lord, I've been wrong. Will You give me another chance?" It's good for us that You are the God of the Second Chance. Sometimes, it takes a third, fourth or fifth chance. Surely, Your mercy is wider and deeper than the sea—wider than the seven seas.

I was one of those so sorely in need of a second chance, just a few short years ago; of course, You know that. Thank You for taking me in your arms of love after I had been away so long; thank You for welcoming me home before You started to instruct me in Your school of loving discipline. The discipline has become fun; now I'm living to the hilt!

Hold fast my hand, Oh God, that I may not slip back into the world I knew, and which can never again offer a thrill comparable to the one I have in walking with Thee.

Monday

JUST had a good massage and rub-down from my fine friend, Anna Vukov of Sherman Oaks. I became so tense in my neck and shoulders, under the strain of hard work, that I could hardly go on. What gentle strength Anna has in those hands of hers!

While she worked on me, I worked on her: I had a chance to tell her again about how You keep me young. I told her I believed You kept me young in body and spirit by giving me lots to do, and that the doing of Your work is the healthiest, most invigorating therapy there is.

I have seen stooped shoulders straightened, and crushing loads removed from tired, old backs, and worry-lines taken out of human faces by the application of that therapy. I have seen pain-wracked bodies straighten up and walk again, and half-crushed souls rise up and sing for sheer joy. Having seen that, I have no reason to "wait for another!"

"He restoreth my soul: he leadeth me in the paths of righteousness for his name's sake. . . ."

Tuesday

AT THE Hollywood Christian Group last night Frances Eilers told me about Dr. Louis Evans' daughter being stricken with polio. It was tremendously inspiring to hear that this brave and beautiful girl was as fine a Christian in her iron lung prison as she had been in the days of her good health. And it was even more inspiring to learn of Dr. Evans' attitude toward this illness of his daughter. Polio is hard to take—not only for the victims, but for those who only stand and watch, and who feel so helpless to do anything to help! Dr. Evans is far from helpless. He says, "These tragic clouds we see are just the dust God is kicking up as He works." If that isn't glorious, then I can't imagine what would be glorious.

How consecrated and dedicated he is! What a spiritual giant! He is one of the most inspiring Christians I know; every time I have had the pleasure of being in his company, he has given me a spiritual boost.

There is healing in Thy hand, Lord; help us to feel it. There is a divine intelligence in Your methods, Lord; make us see it.

Wednesday

OUR good friend Elise Miller Davis has written a grand story about our family. She has done a good job of it, and I have come to admire her ability.

But even more than I admire her ability do I love what she plans to do with her pay-check—she will contribute, by tithing, to research work in mental retardation. My cup just ran over, when I heard that.

So little Robin's ripple of love spreads wider and wider. What a joy and blessing to watch it. And how mighty is the little acorn of love, in helping other little children like our Robin!

"Inasmuch as ye have done it unto one of the least of these, my brethren, ye have done it unto me. . . ."

Thursday

WELL, here we are again at NBC, taping our show. I am writing this between "takes." Cheryl is with us. After the program, Roy and I have to shoot some Christmas and Valentine's Day pictures.

Tomorrow, Roy and I go to court to officially make Mary Little Doe (Dodie) our daughter. The Kentucky court was late in getting Sandy's release papers to us, so we can't legally adopt *him* until Spring. We had wished we could adopt both of them at the same time.

But what difference does it really make, so long as God has led them into our home and our lives? We are so grateful for them; we only pray now that we may lead them as God would have us lead!

"All things work together for good to them that love the Lord . . ." I'll rest on that, Lord!

Friday

DR. HARLEY W. SMITH, rector of St. Nicholas Protestant Episcopal Church here in Hollywood, tells me he is writing the Bishop of London, in England, telling him that Roy and I will be with Billy Graham during the London Crusade for Christ. I'm a little frightened at the thought of meeting such a famous churchman; he must be very stern, and forbidding! But I am glad to have such an introduction to the Church of England; Roy and I are both anxious to study the fascinating history of that Church, right on British soil!

Jesus said, "I am the vine and ye are the branches . . ." and certainly this Church is one of the great branches of the Christian faith. (Maybe some scholars would quarrel with this interpretation of His words, but let them quarrel; that's what it means to me!)

I've been noticing more and more, lately, how some of the branches of the Church stress one part of the gospel, while other branches stress something else. But to me they are all parts of the same body, with Christ as the head. The arms of our human bodies may perform one function, the legs another—but they are all part of just one body. Isn't that the way we should think of the churches, Lord? To think of them in any other way would destroy my faith in all of them.

They keep arguing over doctrine. Why? Why don't we all spend more of our precious time in these desperate days—when men's hearts are fainting from fear—in lifting up Christ? Can't we all do that, whatever Church we belong to? Jesus said bluntly, "And I, if I be lifted up . . . will draw all men unto me."

Honestly, Father, many of our converts become so confused over these doctrinal arguments that they lose sight of the Saviour in the confusion. What good does it do them to have exactly the right "doctrine" if they have no vital Christ? To me, there is only one issue that is all-important: that is that Christ came into this world in the flesh, lived without sin among men and died on the cross to save sinners. Whoever believes that, and follows Him, shall not perish, but have everlasting life. Isn't that the crux of the whole business, Lord? I think it is. If I'm wrong, please tell me, quickly.

And if a person sincerely wants to follow Christ, will not Christ reveal His doctrine, in the Bible, so that that person can understand it? To me, He is His first doctrine, He Himself, and I think we should put first doctrines first!

Your Son has told me that the Comforter, the Holy Spirit, would lead us into all truth. I believe that, Father.

Tuesday

FORGIVE me, Father, for letting the world crowd in on me and so occupy my time that I have not had time for several days to keep up on the spiritual book-keeping in this diary. I didn't forget; I just couldn't seem to get to it.

Of course, that's a silly excuse. I found time to get to the work I thought I *had* to do.

Roy and I are on the train, starting on our way East, and it's such a relief to be where no telephones can ring, and where there is no avalanche of mail facing me every time the postman comes.

Last night I read again that verse in the 84th Psalm which tells of the swallow making her nest on the altar of God. Meditating on that, I thought of the swallows that come back regularly, every year, to Capistrano. I am astonished at that literal fulfilment of the Biblical Psalm; every year, at a certain time in the Spring, the swallows *do* come in droves to nest atop the old San Juan Capistrano Mission in California.

Not a sparrow flies or falls without Your knowledge, without Your direction. People marvel at the "instinct" of those Capistrano swallows, as they keep their schedule of flight and arrival. I wonder if it's instinct? How could the very young birds do some of the things they do? They do those things with no experience whatever! No, I can't stop with calling it instinct. I think You have a hand in directing them. And if You think so much of the sparrows and the swallows, how much more do You think of us, if we have the courage and faith to listen?

In the strangest ways and places, I find Thy Word fulfilled in all that is around me. Truth is still truth, unchanged, unchanging.

Wednesday

Two letters in last week's mail stand out in my mind. One was from a girl writing a test paper in high school, on the adoption of children; the other was from a heartsick, grieving mother who has just lost her little borderline Mongoloid boy. There are so many letters coming in, most of them of a personal nature, and they must be personally and prayerfully answered. I am trying to answer most of them personally, and it is a tremendous task. Thank You for keeping me fit and strong to do it!

Being the wife of a public figure like Roy Rogers, trying to mother five children at home, working in pictures and radio and TV, making personal appearances with Roy and (occasionally) even daring to "mother" him (!) and trying desperately to put You ahead of all of it is no mean job for a country girl like me. Sometimes the pressure is so terrible that I feel I must break under it. I start to flounder, and complain, and then I begin to realize that it's my own fault, and certainly not Yours! Of course You know all about it, and of course You will have me carry whatever burden You think I ought to carry.

If I am trying to do too much, I'm sure you will find a way to slow me down. There's one thing certain: You never send more than we should bear. If we crack up, we're lugging around some luggage that isn't ours.

Keep Thou my feet; I do not ask to see the distant scene; one step enough for me.

Thursday

It's wonderful, the way adopted children walk into one's heart. Pretty soon, you completely forget that they're adopted. They are your very own, and they fill their own niche in your heart. Little Dodie has already been such a blessing to me, and so has Sandy. I think adopted children do more for the parents than the parents could possibly do for them.

A child is the essence of heaven; that is what Jesus thought when He said, "For of such is the Kingdom of Heaven."

When our adopted ones have become curious as to what adoption means, as compared with natural parenthood, I have told them that God has adopted *all* of us—that in Christ we are all God's children. I also tell them that God has given Roy and me the precious privilege of being their earthly guardians. For some reason, it wasn't best for their natural mother to raise them. I've explained that we are all the same in God's eyes; it was He who made us all. Therefore, He is our Father and we are all really brothers and sisters to each other, and if we believe on His Son, Jesus, and try to obey God, we will all live together as angels in heaven at the end of this life on earth. He has left word for us that "In the resurrection there will be no marrying or giving in marriage, but we will be as the angels."

Therefore, I teach our children that the most important thing in their lives is to love God, their Father, above everyone and everything. If I can only get that clearly established in their minds!

Father, I believe that a home not built on the rock of faith hasn't a chance. Help me give my children a chance.

Friday

ROBIN keeps coming back to me; indeed, it is as though she had never left! She's back stronger than ever now, since I have just finished reading a letter from a mother grappling with a week-old grief over the loss of her baby son. That letter struck at my heart. It stirred memories.

I saw myself again walking in the dusk, from the barn to the house, where Roy was waiting for me. Tears were streaming down my face; I had just thanked You for the two glorious years of Robin's life with us; I had said to You, "if it is Your will, Lord, take her." Just as I reached the house, Virginia came up to me and said, "She's gone, Dale."

I guess I cried pretty hard for a few minutes, and then I startled myself by suddenly stopping; I looked at Roy with an incredible peace flooding my soul and a voice whispering, "She's free! Our little Robin is free. No more human limitations now; our little bird can fly. She's dropped her awful braces, and taken wings!"

It's strange but it's true: in that saddest hour, I knew one of the happiest moments of my life!

Into Thy hands, Father, I commend my spirit.
I long for the day when my spirit shall mount
up with wings, as the eagle. . . .

Saturday

ROBIN is still with me, today. So is peace. Father, that "peace which passeth all understanding" is no idle promise, at least to those who put their trust in Jesus Christ.

I never looked at Robin again, after that night. I told Roy I had rather not look at her, because I wanted to remember her beautiful wide blue forget-me-not eyes, and that precious little angelic smile she had.

I have since regretted not seeing her, but (forgive me, Father), I was afraid I would go to pieces and make it harder for everyone else, especially for the children. For their sakes, it was best for me not to crack; it would have left a regrettable impression on them.

To me, anyway, Robin was no longer in that painful flesh; she was active and risen with You.

"Peace I leave with you, my peace I give unto you . . . (so) Let not your heart be troubled, neither let it be afraid."

Sunday

LITTLE ROBIN was buried on her birthday. The funeral was set for four o'clock. Her daddy took her little clothes, picked out the little casket and the crypt at Forest Lawn, and went to see her the night before. Oh, how I struggled with that longing to see her once more, as he walked into the slumber room at Forest Lawn. . . .

When he came out, it was apparent that he had been overcome, but his eyes were shining, and he said, "She's the most beautiful thing I ever saw; one look at her face, and I knew *instantly* where she was. We'll never have to worry about our baby. She's in heaven."

Then I said, "I wish I could be as certain about the future of the rest of our children."

Instantly, in the twinkling of an eye, we shall be changed. . . . What finer treasure could life hold than that one thought?

ON THE day of the funeral, I was having my morning coffee when I looked out of the window at Robin's little house, and the realization that this was her birthday hit me with terrible force.

I fled from the kitchen to my bedroom, and fell on the bed beneath the portrait of Robin. That was a bad squall, Father, with Satan in there and really pitching at me. All I could say was, "Oh Lord, this is Robin's birthday, and she's gone."

Then Ruth (the nurse who had attended Robin the last week with Virginia) came into the room and said, "Dale, there's something I think you should know. Robin had been unconscious since before noon, with her eyes closed. After you kissed her and went off to pray, she opened her eyes wide, looked straight up—not that usual rolling of the eyes, but looking straight up toward the ceiling—and held out her arms, as if to say, 'Here I am, Lord; take me.' Then she stopped breathing, so gently that we could hardly catch the change. Just like a little ship slipping her moorings and gliding silently out to sea."

Father, bless that girl for what she did for me, in that moment. Thank You for the angels You send to stand by in the hour of death. We are often unaware of them, too!

Wednesday

TODAY I've been thinking of how You sent Dodie and Sandy to us. They were the rainbows after the storm.

I left Los Angeles with a heavy heart, missing Robin terribly, that September night, en route for Madison Square Garden. And I came home with not one but two more chicks.

By the time we reached Dallas, *Angel Unaware* was half written. I had two rough moments on that trip—one after boarding the train at Los Angeles, and the other when I saw Robin's picture on my mother's dresser, in Italy, Texas.

As we were booking passage on a plane to take me over to see my brother in Jackson, Mississippi, Roy (bless him!) asked me, "How would you like to adopt another baby?" I said no, there just wasn't a baby anywhere to take Robin's place—and then, for a reason I didn't understand, I said, "But I would like to go by Miss Carson's, at Hope Cottage (a foster-home in Dallas) and just look at the babies." Perhaps I thought it would help me; perhaps God had an idea . . . !

As we came up the steps of Hope Cottage, I remembered that on a previous visit there I had seen a little baby who was part Choctaw Indian. She was then about two months old. I asked the nurse if "that little part-Indian girl" was still there; she replied, "Yes, she is.

She has just finished her tests—and she sure is a winner!" I asked to see her. That did it!

They brought out a bouncing black-eyed baby "with hair like a raven's wing, and a smile like the sun." I practically grabbed her away from the nurse, and held her in my arms. I looked down at her face, and the sun broke through the clouds for the first time in weeks, and everything that was wrong was right again, and life was good, and smiling.

I almost shouted at the nurse, "I've got to have her. May I?" I knew the answer, before I got it. I knew it was no accident that I had come out to Hope Cottage "to see the babies." I was *led* out there, and by no human hand.

In a split second I knew that little Dodie needed me, and that I needed her, and that she was God's answer to my loss of Robin.

You do move in mysterious ways, Lord, Your wonders to perform. Keep me awake to the fact that You do move, and that to You, it's no mystery, but a plan. And thanks again for putting little Dodie in my arms.

Thursday

I'VE been reading over what I wrote yesterday, and thinking again of what Roy said that day at Hope Cottage. I said to him, "She'll never take Robin's place, but she'll have her own place. If they will let us have her, I want her. Do you?" And he said, "Honey, if you want that baby, we'll move the earth out of place to get her. Do I want her? Look—that baby has the same strain of Indian blood in her veins that I have and we ought to hit it off fine. Sure I want her!"

What a guy he is! No wonder people love him. He has a heart as big as the great outdoors; it's big enough for everybody, and he's forever trying to get everybody into it.

I shall never forget how You taught Roy that there is blessing to be had in affliction—even in afflicted children, a sight that had always bothered him up until the time You sent Robin to teach him otherwise. In her he saw, with his own eyes, how You can get into people's hearts through an afflicted child, and make better people of them.

I have seen You do that with Roy; since the advent of Robin, I have been an eye-witness to the most beautiful unfolding of Christian character and purpose that I have ever known, in anyone, anywhere, at any time.

To me, Robin was never an accident of nature. You sent her to work a miracle in her parents.

I've heard Roy say, "There's some reason why the Lord has given me success and permitted me to climb to the top in my field. There are other fellows who can out-sing me, out-act me, and who are much better looking than I'll ever be. Why did He pick me? What's the reason?" Father, I believe You picked him because he was humble, because he was good material for Your hand. You permitted him to have this success—then You "threw the book at him", with the dying of Robin, to temper the steel that was in him. I'm grateful.

If anyone had told me, ten years ago, that I would pick up a TV magazine in a railroad station this morning and read a line written by Roy Rogers: "Without religion and Jesus Christ, there just wouldn't be any meaning in life for me!"—if someone had told me I would *ever* read that about Roy, I'd have said, "You're out of your mind."

Or if anyone had prophesied that I would ever tell the world about my adorable little Mongoloid baby, I'd have said the same thing. . . .

I had too much personal pride and ambition, ten years ago, to foresee such a situation. But You handled it nicely.

You have given us only good, Lord; I can think of nothing bad. . . .

> *"The Lord will give grace and glory; no good thing will he withhold from them that walk uprightly."*

Friday

I HAVE been thinking of Catherine Marshall's talk the other night, at the Hollywood Christian Group. She must be a great help to You, Lord, what with those two books of hers based on the life and work of her husband,

Peter Marshall, and her new ministry of the spoken word as she travels across the country. She showed us how smoothly You can work.

You know, Anna Vukov (my masseuse) said a fine thing that night. She said she had no idea that Hollywood people could pray as they prayed in that meeting; she was almost stunned by the simple faith she saw in the faces and heard in the prayers. She said, "It was so wonderful—seeing rich and poor, alike and equal, in that room."

Of course, it should be that way, *shouldn't* it? Money, position, education, background, color—these are not assets in the Kingdom. Love is the coin of that realm, and fellowship is the equalizer.

> *"Seek ye first the Kingdom of God, and all these things shall be added unto you."*

Saturday

STILL on the train. This is a long trip, with very frequent stop-overs in cities and towns along the route. I enjoy it Lord, but it does take a lot out of me.

Night before last, I came down with a painful throat infection; thought I could never keep a speaking engagement the next day. I felt feverish and as hoarse as a frog. I crawled into bed early, You remember, and for over an hour we talked about it, and asked You to see to it that I could talk next morning, and keep that engagement.

I woke up with a perfect voice, and with the feeling that I could lick a team of wildcats, single-handed.

Now that I think of it, I know why You gave me back my voice. The speaking engagement was to give a short testimony and to do the narration for *Symphony of Life,* a short color film about the creation, fall and redemption of man.

I think You wanted that film completed, for some reason, right away, and no trifle like a sore throat was going to stand in Your way.

". . . and he will teach us of his ways, and we will walk in his paths. . . ."

Sunday

FATHER, what a beautiful sight outside my train window this morning! It took my breath, and made me sing. There were majestic, snow-blanketed mountains over there on the horizon, under a sky that was alternately heavy and gray, and with clouds bursting wide open to reveal the blue beyond, and to let the sun through for a little to bless the snow with sparkling light. No artist could possibly have done it justice; no human hand can even imitate Thine!

Oh, God, You call to me from every common bush along the way!

"He giveth snow like wool; he scattereth the hoarfrost like ashes. He casteth forth his ice like morsels: who can stand before his cold? He sendeth out his word, and melteth them: he causeth his wind to blow, and the waters flow."

Monday

TODAY, I am going to stay in bed—right here in my "bunk." Whatever there is to do, can wait. I intend to take a day off to enjoy Your words of Life and talking with You, and meditating. Mostly, I think, I'll listen.

I should do this more often. Why do I hurry so? Why do we all try to run a four-minute mile to the grave? We rush around like a lot of children playing tag with each other, and all of a sudden God halts one of us and says "It's time for you to stop."

Some folks, I hear, long to make a complete, final break with their work and just go off to a mountain and meditate until they die. I can sympathize with them, but I hardly think that's necessary. If we would only have sense enough to take a day off now and then to get our bearings and rest our souls, and then go back to whatever work we have, we'd find it a lot easier to do.

And, probably, we'd understand then that whatever work we're doing is actually God's work. That ought to make a difference!

"Rest in the Lord, and wait patiently for him; fret not thyself because of him who prospereth in his way . . . ."

Wednesday

ROY and Jim Osborne, our business manager, who is traveling with us, are up in the club car talking over business matters, so I have a few minutes to myself.

How thrilled I was last night to discover that Jim Osborne, too, is a fine Christian and a diligent seeker after Your Truth. It's just one more! Father, when I think of the transformation You've brought about in the whole organization of the Roy Rogers Enterprises, I am overwhelmed. The thinking and acting of all of us has been changed. It keeps unfolding, like a rose, with new petals opening steadily. When I behold thy handiwork . . . !

You have used our personal manager, Art Rush, in a very wonderful way. Before I ever knew Roy Rogers, Art was my radio manager. I was far away from You then, Father. Art knew it, and he used to talk to me about Your goodness and Your ability to guide Your children. He wasn't paid to do that; he just had to.

He used to talk to me about Roy, too. He had such great plans for Roy; he told me frankly that he was trusting You to unfold the plan.

He knew Roy needed a deeper, saving knowledge

of You, but somehow Art could never quite bring it off. You made Yourself known to Roy in another way—through Robin. But I'm not so naive as to think that Art's plugging was wasted, all across those years. He dropped the seed—a lot of seed, into pretty rocky soil, every time he got the chance. He *prepared* the soil.

How wise You were to direct the unsuspecting minds of Roy Rogers and Dale Evans to this wonderful Christian Hollywood agent. Without him, we might still be walking our blind alleys.

> *O the depth of the riches both of the wisdom and knowledge of God! how unsearchable are his judgments, and his ways past finding out!*

Thursday

I WOULD rather have Jesus Christ as my Saviour than to be the smartest and richest atheist in the world.

How can a man be an atheist? Doesn't he know he can't produce life? Let's suppose the scientists *could* make a man of flesh and bone, brain and heart. I would like to see them go on and make those cells replenish themselves correctly. I would like to see them give their man-made creature wisdom and faith!

So man has split the atom. Can he *make* an atom? No, he can only split it, and with it destroy himself and all his works! He is only following in Adam's footsteps, promoting death.

It sickens me to hear America brag about its atom bomb. What security is there in *that?* It is a wicked instrument, and it can mean the end of all of us. We are wicked when we put our faith in it. We need to turn back from the atom to the Almighty. . . .

> *"If my people which are called by my name shall humble themselves . . . and turn from their wicked ways; then will I . . . forgive their sin . . . ."*

Friday

A MAN has said to me, "A crusader who dies for a cause is a fool; he may be wrong. People who rant about causes are fools; they never get any thanks for suffering and dying in a cause, but only abuse."

Of course, they want no thanks for their pains. Jesus didn't go up on the cross just so He might have the satisfaction of hearing some Pharisee shout "Thanks!" He went up there to save men who wouldn't be born for centuries to come. The cause, not the immediate thanks or condemnation, is what is important.

Let men call me foolish for Christ's sake, O God! Keep me from resenting that; it is actually acclaim.

I shall try to hew to Thy line until the end of my run, come what may, sorrow or reward.

I beg of You, Lord, never to let me be caught sitting in the seats of the scornful.

Saturday

FORGIVE me my debts, Lord, and my broken promises.

My conscience swung a mean blow at me today, when I sat thinking of how I would put You first in everything when I thought Tom was stricken with infantile paralysis. I begged You to make him well, for he was just six years old and a blessed little tyke. If You would, I bargained (!)—save him from infantile paralysis, if You would only let that spinal fluid test come out negative, then I'd give You my life. You did Your part, but I didn't do mine. The test came out negative; so did I. Ambition got the upper hand, and I forgot all about the promise.

Thanks for correcting me through Robin. I needed that, and I am grateful for it.

I know now, Father, that we do not bargain with You; we co-operate, or else . . . .

Sunday

HERE it is Sunday morning. The last three days have certainly been hectic, and tiring. What would I ever do without Your strength?

The *Santa Fe Chief* pulled in here at ten thirty—too late for us to get to church, which I regret. We took a cab to the Blackstone Hotel, and when we checked in at the desk Roy was delighted to meet an old friend in the lobby—the well-known writer, H. Allen Smith, and his charming wife.

Allen Smith did a piece on Roy years ago, in *Life Magazine,* when Roy was just beginning to climb the ladder in show business. Mr. Smith teased me about *Angel Unaware* being on the best-seller list. He is such a famous writer that I was a little flustered by his presence, and by his kidding.

As a matter of fact, I was so awed at meeting such a keen wit that I failed to tell him that it was You who wrote *Angel,* and not I. That shouldn't have happened.

In everything I do now, in everything that happens to me or through me, I see myself as a small stream carrying vast mountain snows down to Your great ocean. That's a presumptive comparison, Father, and maybe a bad one. It limits You. But it's the best my finite mind can muster.

What I'm saying is that I am a channel, and no more.

"And a man shall be . . . as rivers of water in a dry place, as the shadow of a great rock in a weary land." Make me like that!

Wednesday

THREE whole days and nights of hustle and bustle! Here it is Wednesday. I've just come from a luncheon with Roy, Elise Davis (our fine writer friend) and a group of men representing the Roy Rogers Enterprises and other men who use the merchandise bearing our label.

I wasn't too anxious to attend that luncheon; it was one of those "strictly business" things, and I thought they could get along without me. For some reason or another I went, and now I'm so glad I went that my heart could burst.

For, You see, we agreed on a new "brand," or label, for our merchandise. It is a "plus" sign. Is it coincidence that this plus sign so closely resembles a cross? Furthermore, "plus" means *added*—and it came over me like a flash that You said, once, "Seek ye first the Kingdom of God and all these things shall be added unto you!"

I can't think of anything finer that could happen

to us, than to have a sign resembling a cross on everything connected with our business. Maybe we have a chance now to tell of the Kingdom through that business, as we never had it before!

I thought, too, as we sat at that luncheon table, of other words of Christ: "I am come that ye might have life and have it more abundantly." I like to think of all life—all my life, at least—as being lived under the plus-sign of the cross.

It's a little thing, this "plus" sign on our stuff, but it is startling. Your cross is forever before my eyes, whatever I do, wherever I go.

Be partner to our business, Lord, even as Thou art unseen companion to us in all else!

Saturday

Two days of furious hurry and work: I've been so busy with our appearances here in Chicago, Lord, that I have cut down my prayer-time. Why is it that when we come through the gates of the Kingdom, we want to pray all the time? Why didn't we feel that way before?

Perhaps I did pray all the time, at that. I found myself praying in the busiest moments of the show, at lunch, hurrying through the streets in a cab, checking up on things before the show started—everywhere!

And I prayed hard during that ride in the big parade down State Street.

What a parade that was! You had it rain hard on Friday night, so the air would be clear and sharp this morning. The air tingled with winter sunshine as Roy and I turned Trigger and Buttermilk, our horses, down State Street. The Chicago folks were standing all along the curb, in their pre-Christmas joy. What wonderful faces they were! I couldn't help thanking You for Christmas, when I looked at them.

And the children! In their little faces I saw curiosity, anticipation, fulfilment, adoration, unbounded delight. Do You know what I was thinking, as I rode along in the midst of their wild cheering? Not of their cheers, Lord; I was thinking of how necessary it is for those of us who are grown to become as little children, in order really to enter the Kingdom of heaven. Some folks may think that's a funny thing for a cowgirl to be thinking as she leads a parade down a city street, but that's what I was thinking, take it or leave it.

Children are such innocent, trusting souls; God, never let me let them down! They look for good, and believe with all their hearts that it will come because You have *promised* it will come. I'm not worried over that aspect of their faith or adoration, for I know You never let anybody down.

What would I do without the sight of children's faces? What would *You* do? Grown-ups betray us, and disappoint us, and make a shambles out of a world You intended to be beautiful, and we're just about ready to give up when along comes another generation, bright-eyed and laughing and with a divine faith that things will work out for the best—and we elderly stumblers and blunderers take hope again, and go on with the fight. Jesus knew what He was talking about when He said that of such were the Kingdom . . . !

Suffer us to come to You with the faith-filled hearts of childhood, with its clean laughter and dreams and its ability to be eternally undismayed.

Sunday (Before Church)

I AM still tired after those two shows yesterday afternoon, following the parade, a rehearsal at the Chicago Stadium for the Harvest Moon Festival, and then the late show at 10:30 P.M. You know, Father, I had a real attack of stage fright when I saw that huge stadium packed to the top. Stage-fright is a show-business term for "self un-triedness," and I think old Satan offers it to us as one of his choice inventions. He sure tempted me with it; he said, "Look, gal. You're pretty tired, and you're hoarse from yelling to all those kids along State Street, so why don't you just give up? If you go out in that Stadium and try to sing that *Somewhere Over the Rainbow* song of yours, your voice will crack on the high notes, sure as my name's Satan. They'll laugh at you. They're tired too, you know; they've been sitting there a long, long time." I almost fell for it.

Then I asked You to help me hit that high note

right on the nose—and You did! You're the No. one antidote for stage fright, in any situation.

What Satan wanted, I think, was for me not to sing that little extra stanza we add after the first chorus:

In a land that's far away,
A little babe was born one day
In a manger;
And if to Him we daily pray
He'll take our load of care away.
To me, He's no stranger.
If we follow the Master, bye and bye,
We'll fly over the rainbow . . .
You can, and so can I!

I know, there has been some criticism of my singing that; some folks don't seem to think that religion has any place in a rodeo, or a show like ours. Well, if it hasn't, then I'm through with shows and rodeos! I won't go where I can't take God.

They got the message, while we sang. Many, many people came up to me, afterwards, and talked with me about it; they were so thankful. And at the midnight reception later, atop the Sherman Hotel, a lot more of them spoke of it. It clicked. I'm glad I sang it. I'll sing it again, and again, and again, so long as I have breath, and the devil's fifth column can just go chase itself.

I think there is something inherently public in the word "witnessing." What right has any man or woman to keep his faith "strictly private?"

Sunday (Later)

THIS morning George Wilson, who is Billy Graham's business manager, took Elise Davis and me to Moody Church to hear the new pastor, Dr. Redpath. What a preacher he is, and what a blessing to my soul! Every day should be Sunday, and every preacher should have that man's fire!

He preached on "The Walls of Jericho"—on how people had to be silent, in so many difficult situations, and "encompass the city," and wait for Your orders before they sent up their shouts of triumph. What a lesson in obedience! We need to learn to *wait* on You, Lord, and not to rush on You with all sorts of demands. That's a bad failing of mine. I'm impatient, and You aren't, and too often I get into trouble trying to change Your schedule. I must stop that . . .

Give me the grace and the decency to be still,
and to know that You are God.

WHAT a privilege it was to see little Jimmy J—— this morning. His mother wrote and explained to us that Jimmy was ill with a dangerous pancreatic inflammation, and—could we possibly come and see him, just for a minute? Roy just couldn't get away. When he called Jimmy's mother, after talking with her on the phone, she cried; so did Roy, when he hung up. Ever since You took Robin home, Roy seems to see her in every afflicted child.

Thanks to You, I was able to go. I'll never forget it. I couldn't deny that mother's plea; she had promised Jimmy during one of his violent attacks, that when we came to town she'd try to get one of us to come and see him, and she didn't want the boy to lose faith in her promise.

We talked and laughed and prayed, and I know we all felt that You were in the room with us. It was the high spot of our whole Chicago experience.

The letters we get from people like Jimmy's mother break our hearts over and over—just as the wounds in Christ's hands must be broken open afresh, constantly, as He comes in contact with human suffering. I think we should all tune our ears more carefully to the agony of God as He sees pain, and in His name do what we can to heal it. What else are we here for?

Never let me become so busy, Lord, that I become careless of a chance to serve.

Tuesday

THE Christmas season is starting, and I am beside myself with the joy of it. Right now, Your Kingdom of holy purpose and righteousness looms up before me in a strange, vast, illimitable way, and I'm like a tot seeing his first Christmas tree. I see a huge tree, bulging with the most delicious things, and I'm just "zealous" enough, and "peculiar unto Christ" enough, to want to eat every bit of it. The trouble is that I want to eat it all at once, so You'll have to restrain me, Father.

On the train coming into New York, Roy and I read a book given us by Mrs. George Wilson—it is *The Christian's Secret of a Happy Life,* by Hannah Whitehall Smith. We literally feasted on it. To think it was written in 1870, and that nearly two million people have bought it and read it, across the years! Why, it could have been written yesterday! (Just goes to show you that Your truth is ageless, timeless, and eternal).

Roy told me this morning that he had an amazing experience on one page of this book. He said the author showed him what to *do* to gain victory through Christ. Roy said he had never really claimed that victory, and that he had struggled against terrific odds to get it. But last night, reading the book, he saw for the first time that we do not *attain* this victory; we *obtain* it as the gift of Jesus Christ. That's a startling thought.

Roy remarked to me, in a voice so low I could hardly hear it, that You were stirring him up inside, and that You must be getting him ready for something. He didn't just know *what* was happening, but he felt it!

He says that he stopped in the middle of a chapter and asked You to take his life, twist it, break it if necessary, but to re-form it and use it for Your glory. It makes me feel so small, Lord—it took me about twenty-five years to ask You to do that for me! Even with a Christian childhood behind me, it took a quarter of a century—and Roy "came to terms" with the great challenge in five short years.

How mighty and resounding is the still small voice!

"O Love that will not let me go, . . .
I rest my weary soul in thee;
I give thee back the life I owe,
That in thine ocean depths its flow
May richer, fuller be."

Wednesday

OUR good friends, Dr. Norman Vincent Peale, and Frank Mead and Wilbur Davies of the Fleming H. Revell Company (they published *Angel Unaware*) have just left; they came up for breakfast with us, in our hotel room. What a delightful time we had together! They are valiant soldiers of the Kingdom, fighting on different fronts. We talked of the trials and tribulations of being Christian in these days, and we had a good laugh over a lot of them! These men have a great sense of humor. They can laugh off the most devastating criticism of their books and sermons, and that is a gift straight from God! They are serious enough when the criticism is important, but stupid or intolerant criticism they throw off like so many ducks shedding water off their backs! I cherish the gift of good humor in the faith. There would be a lot fewer spiritual casualties, if we had more of it.

We discussed the problem of publishing religious books—of how hard it is to get a book published that will find any audience at all, with people in the churches so divided and quarrelling among themselves. I think I'd rather write books than publish them, for the publishers seem to be sitting on a keg of dynamite that never quite goes off, but that *could* go off at any minute.

Dr. Peale has the answer, I think; he says, "Write what God gives you to write, and forward all letters of criticism to Him!" That makes good sense to me.

I don't think I shall try to write to please anyone but Him. I think He would detest any other kind of writing!

Help me to write and speak in courage and in candor, O God, never to flatter but always to witness to the best and noblest I have found in Thee.

STILL thinking of our conversation at yesterday's breakfast. . . .

Maybe I'm wrong in expecting complete unity among Christians. After all, there are bound to be differences of opinion in theology and religion—particularly in the Protestant department, where differences created our churches. No two human minds are the same, no two pairs of human eyes ever see the same thing.

The Master said, "I am the vine, *and ye are the branches*—and no two branches are ever the same, either!

What bothers me is the bitter competition that has developed among the branches of the Church. If the branches of any tree were to fight each other so, the tree would die in short order! I don't mean to "harp" on this, Father, but I am more and more concerned about it, as I travel around the country and see its disastrous effects. It grieves me to see Christians shutting off the flow of divine blessing with their little hand-made dams of contention.

If the life-giving "sap" of the Vine is cut off, what happens to the branches?

Why can't we concentrate on the *positive* aspects and fruits of Christian faith? Why can't we all stand together and say together, "Praise the Lord for what He has done for all of us! He has given us peace of mind (when we accept it!), blessings unlimited here on earth and eternal life hereafter!"

How much have we gained out of the great common heritage of Christian faith. The free schools we cherish began in the Church. The whole vast concept of freedom among all manner of men began with the spiritual freedom brought to us in the person of Christ. Our democracy is rooted in the Christian faith. The hospitals to which we go for healing had their start in the Church.

And above it all is the life-giving faith that at the heart of the universe there is a kindly, loving, forgiving God who will not let us fall or die! That underlies the mighty dignity of man. Without it, we would still be slaves in a Dark Age!

I think I must search my Scriptures, today and tomorrow, for proof of this.

I am grateful, Father, that Thou hast made of one blood all the nations of men; and I am even more grateful that Thou hast put one great Holy Spirit within the reach of all men in all nations.

Friday

I'VE found it, God! Sitting in the railroad station, waiting for the train, I read from First Peter:

For so is the will of God, that with well doing ye may put to silence the ignorance of foolish men: As free, and not using your liberty for a cloke of maliciousness, but as the servants of God. Honour all men. *Love the brotherhood.* (That takes in all the branches, doesn't it, Lord?) Fear God. Honour the king. Servants, be subject to your masters with all fear; not only to the good and gentle, but also to the froward. For this is thankworthy, if a man for conscience toward God endure grief, suffering wrongfully. For what glory is it, if, when ye be buffeted for your faults, ye shall take it patiently? but if, when ye do well, and suffer for it, ye take it patiently, this is acceptable with God. For even hereunto were ye called: because Christ also suffered for us, leaving us an example, that ye should follow his steps: Who did no sin, neither was guile found in his mouth: Who, when he was reviled, reviled not again; when he suffered, he threatened not; but committed himself to him that judgeth righteously. (I Peter 2:15-23.)

I think that's it. I am memorizing it, so that I shall never be far from its beauty and influence.

Can't we all somehow concentrate on that, Father? Is there a Christian who could not "subscribe" to this? Is there a Christian who *should* not?

On Christ, the solid rock, I stand; all other ground is sinking sand!

Monday

I'M WRITING in retrospect now, trying to put down what has happened in the past few days. We're on a plane, speeding toward sunny California. Yesterday, in Detroit, we landed in a snowstorm. This morning the sun is out in all its glory. Thank You for giving us the exhilaration of change from storm to peace, O God. Thank You for sun and snowstorm. It is good that life is so vastly different, from day to day.

What a thrill it was to ride horseback down the street in Philadelphia to Independence Hall. That was on Thanksgiving Day. I shall never forget the joy on the faces of the thousands of free Americans along the way.

As in Chicago, I found myself thinking deep, deep thoughts as we rode along. What a blessing it is to live in a country that is so *free*! How careless we are of our freedoms—freedom of speech, freedom of the press, and above all freedom of worship! I don't think I could live where those freedoms did not exist; I don't believe I could breathe. . . .

When we stood there in the Square looking up at Independence Hall, I thought of the Rock of Gibraltar. There it stands, immovable as a mountain! When I turned to look at the massed people around us, so warmly dressed and happy and kind, it just didn't seem possible to me that anyone would want to change our American way of life. America believes in freedom and justice for all—and that has its roots in Jesus Christ!

I thought of how He said, "Know the truth, and the truth shall make you free." And I thought of the Declaration of Independence, signed within these walls; that document was built on Thy truth, Lord! And I thought of the Constitution; the great freedoms granted and published there would never have been possible had You not first struck from men's souls the shackles of fear and ignorance and bigotry.

"The just shall live by faith." That, too, is in our blood, as Americans. It came down to us from our founding fathers, who first prayed in faith and then acted on the faith. I'm glad I'm an American, Father.

But make me not too glad, or too blindly proud of our past, that I fail to see that we stand in terrible need, right now, of getting back to the principles of the Truth Eternal which gave us birth. Oh, that this Truth might grip all our hearts again, and bring us face to face with the true values of life. Our bodies are indeed well-clad, and well-fed. Feed Thou our souls!

> *"For the nation and kingdom that will not serve thee shall perish. . . . Righteousness exalteth a nation: but sin is a reproach to any people. . . ." May Thy Holy Spirit be upon us as a nation, Lord!*

Monday (Later)

How I enjoyed seeing my old friend Fran Allison, in Philadelphia! She and Burt Tilstrom rode with us in the parade. And her husband, Archie Leventan, too; he took my picture astride good old Buttermilk, in the parade.

Fran is with the "Kukla, Fran and Ollie" TV show, and also on Don McNeil's Breakfast Club show, so she is certainly keeping busy. We laughed over some of the experiences we had together doing our old "Sister Emmy and Cousin Myrtle" hill-billy radio show in Chicago, years ago. We had a lot of fun harmonizing (I use the word loosely!) those old high-pitched songs. Old friends are best, I think.

It was fun, with Fran; we faced something serious when we walked into the home of our friends, in Detroit. We found Dotty Newburg on her knees on the floor, with her arms around little three-year-old Skippy, who had just fallen down stairs. I looked almost in panic at Roy; I was thinking of the tragic fall of little Jo-Ellen Holcomb—Jack Holcomb's daughter—in Waco, Texas, and my heart was terrified lest the same sort of tragedy should be here. Then You spoke to me, and I quieted down.

How wonderful it is to have You around at times like these! You seemed so close in that bedroom, while they were taking X-rays of Skippy's head. Thank You, blessed Father for protecting that little child in his fall. The X-rays showed him to be free of concussion.

Skippy's daddy is one of the big key men in the automobile industry. Help him now, Father, as he faces a crisis that comes, sooner or later, to all manner of men! I enjoyed his stories at dinner, when he told of his wonderful boyhood on a Washington ranch. It was quite like Roy's story. It made me think of Abraham Lincoln, too: what a blessing in disguise is a humble beginning. It seems to get a boy off to a better start in life because a poor boy isn't loaded down with so many "things," right off the bat. Too many things can make a child into a selfish little prig, and a very unhappy man.

It makes me wonder about how we are treating *our* children, and what we are giving them. Father, forgive us if we lean over backwards, sometimes, in not giving our children too many things. It's because we know that material things will never make them happy; that they can stifle the spirit, and create mental confusion, and result in a sense of frustration.

It bothers me. Show us how to give our children more love instead of many things.

Make us poor, for Christ's sake, and determined to seek the Kingdom whether we ever get "all these things," or not!

Tuesday

THANK You, Father, for a wonderful ride through the air. We "set down" at Los Angeles Municipal Airport at 8:05; we were met by Art Rush and Mike North, Art's assistant. We were home!

How glad I was to turn in the drive at "Roger's Rancho," and to tip-toe in to see my sleeping kiddies, Dodie, Sandy and Dusty. I stood over them and thanked You for them.

Coming home to Thee must be like this: pure, unadulterated joy. Why do so many seem to fear it? I look forward to meeting You in heaven just as I looked forward to coming home to Dodie, Sandy and Dusty.

All things turn home at even-tide: Oh God,
let me turn gracefully!

Sunday

SUNDAY! Almost a week since I've written a line in this diary.

Dodie, the two boys and I went to Sunday school today (Cheryl and Linda were spending the week-end with Nana and Granddaddy Wilkins). Then Roy and I went to church and heard a marvelous sermon on Jesus and the money-changers in the porch of His Temple in Jerusalem. It was a perfect sermon for this pre-Christmas season, especially in the way the preacher applied it to us, in our own times.

He showed us that every once in a while a good housecleaning is necessary in our personal, human "temples," where God houses His Holy Spirit. We need to sweep our houses clean, as Jesus swept that porch clean of the money-changers,—clean of the dust of worldly accumulations—before we can appreciate the real joy of Christmas. That's especially true of Christmas, which seems to be just about 100 percent commercialized.

How stupid and blasphemous it is to think that we can *buy* that Christmas joy and good will! It seems shameful to me to worry about how much money we can "afford" to spend at Christmas. Here is Jesus, humbling Himself to be born in a manger, offering us His very life on Calvary for our redemption, and we babble about the "cost" of Christmas! We crowd Him into a few little carols; we over-stuff ourselves with turkey on Christmas Day, and think we're very righteous and good if we just give a Christmas donation to the poor, and offer a prayer before Christmas dinner.

These things aren't wrong; they just aren't *enough*. It must make Jesus turn His face away in humiliation, that we have missed it so. Our minister said, "Why don't we make it a *real* Christmas, and use this season to draw nearer to our Lord, through thankfulness, penitence, meditation and prayer—and distribute our gifts in a Christ-filled spirit, calculating the value of the gift in the light of the Love which gave us the first Christmas?"

It may be a tall order, but we need to see and practice Christmas like that, just as Jesus found it necessary to sweep the money-changers from the Temple porch . . . We need a lot of housecleaning.

"Purge me with hyssop, and I shall be clean; wash me, and I shall be whiter than snow."

Monday

I HAVE just read Mark 3: "And the Pharisees went forth, and straightway took counsel with the Herodians, how they might destroy him. But Jesus withdrew himself and his disciples to the sea: and a great multitude from Galilee followed him, and from Judea."

The call to withdraw, and be silent in Thy presence! Every once in a while Jesus found that necessary. So should we, if we have any sense at all. But no—we let the world hem us in, with its iron curtains of noise, confusion and bewilderment, until peace takes wings and flies away.

I felt that today. Got up early, to have breakfast with the children and see them off to school; I meant to have a quiet hour with You, right after breakfast, before the daily grind got under way. And there was so much noise and confusion that I didn't get a minute for that until 12:15! The washing machine blew a fuse, which meant that our laundry lady couldn't get to work. Dodie fell and cut her nose. The phone rang incessantly. The day *started* wrong, and everything insisted upon going wrong all day long.

But I got that hour in; I went out to the barn, when the children were finally off to school, and the washing-machine fixed, and read Your Word for an hour. We can find the time, if we want it!

I'm afraid I have a "Martha complex." I can understand why Jesus talked the way He did to Martha when she grumbled about Mary failing to put the household task first: He knew that a quiet relationship with Him would smooth out the furrowed brow of the most harassed home-maker.

> *Help me, God, to make a more determined effort to at least start each day by talking intimately with You, before I wade into the rushing stream of daily chores.*

Thursday

WE ARE putting our radio show on tape today; between scenes, let me record a miracle that has just happened.

On the plane from Detroit to Chicago I told Elise Davis about a screen test I had made while I was under contract to 20th Century Fox Studios. The talent coach, Tom Moore, gave me a poem called "The Hound of Heaven," by Francis Thompson. He said I had a spiritual quality in my face, and he thought the poem "suited" me. I didn't quite know what he meant by that until I had read and pondered the poem. It was a poem about running away from God—and it sure *did* suit me.

When I read the poem as part of the screen test, I stumbled over its strange words and meanings—just the way I was stumbling through life. Small wonder the tests that day didn't impress the producers! The test flopped, badly.

That was eleven years ago. Just a month ago, someone sent me a little book of poems, as a gift; leafing through it, my eye fell on "The Hound of Heaven,"—and the message of that amazing verse leaped out of the book right into my heart. For the first time, I got it!

As I was telling Elise about that experience, she said, "I should like to read that poem. Will you lend me that book?" Of course I would. But—search as I would in my library, I just couldn't find it. Next morning I called Mike North; Mike is now Art Rush's assistant and he was my leading man in that screen test eleven years ago! I asked Mike to locate Tom Moore, if he could, and unearth a copy of "The Hound of Heaven." Mike got Mrs. Moore on the phone.

Mrs. Moore said, "Why, what a coincidence! Tom was taking a stroll along the beach just a few days ago, and he found some books that had been washed ashore—from who knows where? He examined the 'lot,'—and he found a tattered old book of poems, among them 'The Hound of Heaven!' He said to me, 'Why, that's the poem I gave Dale Evans to read in her screen test, eleven years ago. I think I'll take it home, and put it on my shelf.' "

Tom called me later, and dictated the poem over the phone.

How You keep after us, God! Eleven years is as nothing, when You are seeking a soul. You caught up with me through a book washed up from the sea!

I think of David saying to Saul: "thou huntest my soul to take it." God says the same to me, in a fairer, sweeter way. He is the eternal Hunter, never giving up!

I shall not rest, Oh Father, until at last I rest in Thee, until I find peace in giving Thee my hunted, haunted soul.

Wednesday

LAST night it was my turn to handle the Hollywood Christian Group program, and I told them about the miracle of Tom Moore, "The Hound of Heaven," and the sea. I read them the poem. I think I'd better put it down here, so I will always have it available.

In this first verse of it is an incredible picture of me running from You, for so many long, long years:

I fled Him, down the nights and down the days;
  I fled Him down the arches of the years;
I fled Him down the labyrinthine ways
  Of my own mind; and in the midst of tears

I hid from Him and under running laughter.
Up vistaed hopes I sped;
And shot, precipitated
Adown titanic glooms of chasméd fears,
From those strong Feet that followed, followed after.
But with unhurrying chase
And unperturbéd pace,
Deliberate speed, majestic instancy
They beat—and a Voice beat
More instant than the Feet—
"All things betray thee, who betrayest Me."

(By permission of The John Lane Company, London)

Friday

FATHER, my heart is so full right now that I can't stand it. You have given me too much today.

Today, the Parents of Retarded Children group, here in the Valley, presented me with an "Award for Outstanding Achievement." It was, they said, for effort on behalf of retarded children and for the publication of *Angel Unaware*. It went deep into my heart, and my eyes filled with tears, and I pretty nearly came "all unglued" again.

You see, I see little Robin in every retarded child.

I'm going to put the Award up on the wall, next to Robin's etching, next to the card beside her picture that says, "All things work together for good to them that love God."

This Award, I think, belongs not so much to me as to five others: first, to You, my Saviour, Who loved the world enough to give Yourself for us on the cross; second and third, to my mother and father, who took so literally the words, "Bring up a child in the way he should go, and when he is old he will not depart from it"; fourth, to my son Tom, who spoke the right word to me at the right time; and fifth, my blessed Robin, the pure flame of sanctification, who turned my feet forever heavenward.

May my outstanding achievement finally be that I have tried my best to follow Thee, and never lost a chance to help others follow.

Saturday

SPEAKING of Robin, Father, may I beg Your forgiveness for criticizing those people who keep going to cemeteries after losing a loved one? For years I was cynical about that; I could never understand why people went out to sit by a grave. I used to ask, "What can they be thinking of? Their loved one isn't there!" I still believe that way, and yet so often my heart is pulled to that little crypt at Forest Lawn. Sometimes for days I cannot rid myself of a feeling of grief and loneliness for my baby. After two or three days of it, I just *have* to go out to that cemetery.

And yet—and here's the wonderful part of it—the minute I walk into that mausoleum and up to her crypt, the weight lifts from my heart and my soul sings and she seems to be there with me! While I am quite aware of the little blue casket behind the bronze plaque, her *spirit* seems to surround me, and *that* has nothing to do with the little human shell resting there!

"Lo, I am with you alway, even unto the end . . . ."

Monday

BAD news today. Kathleen, Roy's youngest sister, has lost her baby.

Thank You, God, for sparing Kathleen's life. Thank You for standing by her and giving her the knowledge that there is a good reason for all this. I pray her husband will understand, too. Make them both aware of Your Presence at the little funeral tomorrow. May they slip their hands in Yours, for keeps.

And thank You for reminding me that there are always others suffering my sorrow, and others who need me.

Make me strong to help them, until the day break and the shadows flee away.

Tuesday

I CAN'T get over the manner in which You take the most unlikely people and use them for Your purpose.

You take folks from the top of the ladder of this world's success, and failures from the bottom, and fuse them into great spiritual weapons. You take half-wayers, drunkards, dope addicts, prostitutes, brilliant intellectuals, down-and-outers and up-and-outers, and make them over in thine own image.

I believe in miracles, for I see miracles worked in human clay, day after day after day!

> *The blind receive their sight, and the lame walk, the lepers are cleansed, and the deaf hear, the dead are raised up, and the poor have the gospel preached to them. What greater miracles could happen, God?*

Thursday

WE ARE getting ready to fly to London the first of next month. It will be quite a scramble. It will take a lot out of us—but what greater joy could we ask than this chance to work with Billy Graham in the London crusade?

It will be a combination working-and-witnessing trip through England, Scotland and Ireland. We will be "on tour" with our show for several weeks, winding up in London just as Billy's campaign is in full swing. We'll do whatever we can, then, to help him.

But I'm not waiting until we get to London to say a good word for Jesus Christ: I'll do that in every show, or know the reason why!

I was looking at little Dodie tonight, and telling myself how hard it would be to leave her. Then I thought of how good it is that You let us have her! Both her, and Sandy. He has grown five inches and put on thirteen pounds this year, and Dodie is something! When she puts her hands over her eyes and mumbles her own little grace at dinner, she makes your heart glow. She's a spunky little thing; those black eyes ("olive eyes," Elise Davis calls them) flash like lightning.

I sing *Jesus Loves Me* to her over and over; she's getting it, gradually. I pray that she gets a complete understanding of Your love, gradually, too.

Thanks again for children, God. They spread Your love around the world. How often are they better witnesses than we adults!

"Suffer the little children to come unto me . . . ."
Suffer me to bring them to You!

I'M TIRED, and sleepy, but before I turn in I want to thank You for the wonderful dream I had last night. Or was it a vision?

I dreamed of an angel hovering over my bed, with her hand on my lips, cautioning me to be silent. There was a glorious light all over the house. I asked my neighbors, in the dream, if they had seen the light, and they said, "Yes. It was caused by the rain glistening on the wings of the angel." Dusty was there, too.

What does it mean, Lord? I don't understand it. Is it that this angel was cautioning me not to talk so much? Or telling me not to tell Sandy something?

I know: I should practice more silence and meditation. Stand guard at my lips, Father. Make me speak when I should speak, and then be silent. And . . .

May the words of my mouth and the meditations of my heart be pleasing in Thy sight.

WHAT a sight from our back porch today! There is fresh snow topping the mountains. I stood there awhile and lifted up mine eyes unto the hills, from whence cometh my help—and I felt strengthened. I thank God for hills and mountains.

Perhaps I needed the sight of those eternal hills this morning. For last night we had an earthquake. You certainly shook us up with that one! Yet, strange as it sounds here, I wasn't afraid when the walls of the house moved, for I knew You were just moulding the clay and revising the earth's pattern a little. I actually enjoyed feeling Your illimitable power in that quake.

I'm not boasting of my courage. But I know I would have been afraid of that earthquake if it had come in the old days, before I came to know You so well. Knowing You has driven fear from me, like tumbleweed before the wind.

"For in the time of trouble he shall hide me in his pavilion: in the secret of his tabernacle shall he hide me; he shall set me upon a rock." . . . It's great to live in a world like that, Father!

I READ in Isaiah: "For thus saith the high and lofty One that inhabiteth eternity, whose name is Holy; I dwell in the high and holy place, with him also that is of a contrite and humble spirit, to revive the spirit of the humble, and to revive the heart of the contrite ones." That fits me like a glove, right now, for the old frustration has caught up with me again. Perhaps frustration isn't just the word; maybe it should be confusion. The old confusion of being so busy that I miss out on moments of prayer and quiet with Thee. Why does life have to be such a furious chase?

For the last two days I haven't been able to start the morning with that necessary "quiet time." By the time I did get around to it, my mind had become an octopus, throwing out its arms in all directions at once. St. Paul must have been rebelling as I am rebelling now, when he said, "For that which I do I allow not: for what I would, that do I not; but what I hate, that do I." It isn't exactly that I hate what I do every day, in my work; it is just that it seems to get in the way of something I want to do more!

May I have patience, God—the sort of patience Jesus had when He looked down from His cross and saw the world mocking Him.

STILL thinking of the verse in Isaiah. Particularly, about the humility and contrite parts. Bible verses can be almost annoying, at times; they get stuck in the mind like an apple paring in the teeth, and they won't budge.

Keep annoying me with that verse, please; I need it. I shed humility sometimes, like a cloak. I need more patience, and more love for my neighbor. How You stressed all that, during Your earthly ministry!

In every person You put here is a Light. Too often we let the fogs of human activity hide that light from our own eyes. Like the "smog" we have in Los Angeles, it just drifts in without a sound, and hides everything! I need You to clear the smog for me, so I can see my neighbor clearer, and know that the Light is still there.

It's our business, I think, to let Thy warmth and light shine through us, to dispel whatever fog or smog there is, so that we can see the Light shining in the other person, too!

In Thy light shall we see light ....

TONIGHT, Roy and I hope to get out to the lovely new home of Henrietta Mears, who has just told me over the phone that she has already dedicated the house to You. She would! The whole house of her life has already been dedicated to You. What a disciple she is!

We've known her for years as Director of Christian Education at The Hollywood Presbyterian Church, where she has so deeply influenced the lives of a multitude of children and young people. But she seems closer to us through her work with Hollywood show people. What understanding she has shown with them! She has turned many a pair of Hollywood feet Christward, and for that we are more than grateful.

There are perfectly good church folks, Lord, who just give us up as a bad job. They seem to ask, "What good can come out of Hollywood?" They seem to think that we are all the hopeless children of the devil—unworthy of anything but contempt and criticism. They just turn us over to the devil—and he has made a devil's own job of some of us!

Hollywood is a continuous field day for Satan. He'd have it easy, if it weren't for people like Henrietta Mears. How he must writhe when she goes to work!

What good can come out of Hollywood? What good came out of Nazareth?

Never let me put up a fence against anyone, God—and keep me from putting a fence around myself!

Friday

IT WAS funny, this morning, when Art Rush called me and asked if I had read the two scripts we were to use on our radio show today. I said, "No. I'll read them when we rehearse. Just haven't had time to read them yet." He seemed concerned that there might be something I wouldn't like, in my lines. I told him to relax—that my days of worrying about that sort of thing were over. If there was anything wrong with those lines, God would tell me in time.

How concerned I used to be about all that—even about the placing of my name as a "star" at the head of the cast—about the little details of the performance. And particularly about the pay-check! The press notices I got, and the part I was given to play—these seemed more important to me then than anything else in the world. What a prison that was!

I was imprisoned by my own ego. It was terrible. Thank You, it's gone now, gone like snow in the sun. Dale Evans has evacuated that house, and Your Holy Spirit has moved in.

Every now and then the ghost of that old Dale Evans comes around, and I get a good laugh. I just say,

"Go away. I don't believe in ghosts." And away it goes, like a scared tramp.

I feel like Alice in Wonderland—only better, because *my* wonderland is real.

All my life I searched for the pot of gold at the foot of the rainbow; now I've found it at the foot of the cross.

> *"Therefore if any man be in Christ, he is a new creature; old things are passed away; behold, all things are become new."*

Friday (One Week Later)

HERE we are in Jackson, Mississippi; we have just left Roy's sister, Kathleen, and her husband, Ted, and I tried to do or say something to help them understand the loss of their baby, little Delia Sue.

I find myself over and over again thanking You for sparing Kathleen's life—but I know how hard it is for her to see things as I do. It is terribly hard for a mother to struggle through childbirth, only to find the little one so crippled and weak that she can live but one day! That's a tough one, Father.

But this I believe, with all my heart: *that someone was made better by the experience.* I cannot believe that You blunder in sending us death. I don't understand Your ways, but I accept them.

You who flung the planets into space have the right to adjust things as You want them; I do not question Your wisdom. I pray for Kathleen that she may have the same understanding about Delia Sue that I have about Robin.

People often ask me, "How did you *get* the understanding you have about Robin?" The answer is easy: "I trusted God to give it to me, and He did."

My heart breaks every time something like this happens—breaks, I think, because I am always so desperately anxious to have these other sorrowing ones healed as You healed me!

> *"But unto you that fear my name shall the Sun of righteousness arise with healing in his wings. . . ."*

Sunday

MY BROTHER said on the way to church this morning, "Sis, the way you read the Bible all the time, you ought to know it by heart!" Know it all, by heart? We *never* know it! The Bible impresses me as the Rocky Mountains impress me: every time I look at it, I see something new.

Someone said recently that "Astronomies change, the stars never." Our ideas change, but Thou—never! Just when we think we have it all figured out, we come on some new idea in the Book, on some "new undiscovered country" between the lines, that we never knew was there, and the whole thing takes fire again.

There is always new Light breaking from it. It is an inexhaustible spring with water ever sweet. I expect to explore it until I die, and still leave great unexplored areas for my children.

Let me die seeking, God!

Monday

SPEAKING of the children, we called them last night, in California. Dodie was cute; she mumbled right into the mouthpiece, and Virginia, her nurse, said she was grinning from ear to ear. She tugged at my heart, by long distance!

They all tug at my heart. I am humbled by them, inspired by them, and I covet great futures for them. Never was a woman so blessed with children!

First, there is Tom, who has brought me safely into the harbor. Then Cheryl, sweet, pretty, talented, filled with zest for life, ambitious enough to keep me on my toes trying to keep her from some of the pitfalls I know so well. There's Linda Lou, the homemaker—kind, watchful for the welfare of others, truly Christian, easily hurt and completely lovable. And Dusty, handsome, blonde, just as shy as his Dad was as a youngster and looking enough like Roy to be a carbon copy; good at sports, with a keen mind, hard to "get to" but soft and sweet underneath. Sandy reminds me of Robin, with his blue eyes, blonde hair and fair skin—a heart as big as all outdoors, still a little insecure but gaining confidence fast. Sandy talks much with me about You; maybe we have a preacher here.

Then there's Dodie, our little "fireball," with eyes flashing one minute and melting the next—black hair like midnight, quick little hands and feet, dancing one second and rushing into bed the next. She drops to the floor and "bites the dust" at an unexpected noise; she mumbles her prayers in her cupped brown hands. She "never misses a trick"; she can "stare you down" with the most intense, level gaze I have ever encountered.

What's Dodie's mission, Father? She has an amazing capacity for love. If it be Your will, I pray that she will be used in a glorious way to help her people, the American Indians.

But *You* guide them wherever You want them to go, Lord; I'll just see that they meet You, and that they eat the true bread of life.

Keep me asking myself, constantly, "What manner of child shall this be?"

Tuesday

WE'RE on our way to New York now—and to Scotland and England. But more than Scotland and England, right now, I am thinking of last Sunday, when my brother and his wife joined the church, in Jackson. It was an answer to my mother's prayers, over the years.

My mom believed Your promise that if a child were brought up Your way, he would not depart from it when he grew older. Six years ago I came back to You, in response to her prayer, and now my brother.

When we said "Good by," at the Jackson airport, my eyes were filled with tears but my heart was singing, and my spirit was crying, "All is well; you are home together spiritually, no matter what happens to you on this earth."

I always rejoice like this when I see anyone join Your church. To me, it is a mighty important step; it can mean the changing of one's whole life, if one takes it seriously enough.

"I love thy church, O God!
Her walls before thee stand,
Dear as the apple of thine eye,
And graven on thy hand."

Wednesday

READ something today that I must get down here. A little item in a magazine . . . It seems that a trainer of Seeing-Eye dogs told his blind companion, as he crossed the street with her guide dog, *"Walk closer to him."*

Maybe that's why I'm so lyrical about people joining the Church. It means walking closer to Him—the only way to walk safely through this life!

> *"And this is love, that we walk after his commandments. This is the commandment, as ye have heard from the beginning, ye should walk in it."*

Thursday

HAVE a sharp pain in my chest, under my ribs. I wonder why. What have I done? Is it nothing, or is it a warning for me to slow down? Wish I knew.

This I do know: You'll take care of it. Maybe You will sweep it away some night while I sleep; maybe You will need the helping hand of one of Your doctors. Either way—why should I worry? It will pass, as every thorn in the side passes.

> *Let me have a thorn occasionally, Father—not that I enjoy the pain, but that it may slow me down long enough to think more of You.*

I'M A little behind with this diary . . . Yesterday Roy presented the National Safety Trophy to the winning school in Fort Worth. The youngsters in that school had the happiest faces! Partly, I suppose, they were happy at the sight of Roy, whom so many of them adore; and partly it was the pride of winning.

Faces glow in victory. I've seen them glow with an unbelievable radiance when Christ has won a victory in the hearts behind the faces! I have seen ugly, dissipated, bitter, discouraged faces transformed almost immediately under Your touch into mirrors of beauty and joy. It is life's highest experience. I crave it for every youngster in the land, and for every grown-up youngster!

The glory that was seen on the face of Jesus Christ—may it be reflected in my face, and on the face of mankind everywhere.

Wednesday

IT's hard to believe, but we're here in *London.* The flight over the Atlantic, in the huge British plane, was glorious. We had nice comfortable berths, in which we were supposed to *sleep*! Not me! I was so excited I couldn't close my eyes.

The plane bounced a little, now and then, in a wild rough wind. You know, I had the sensation of being suspended up there, between the sea and the heavens, in the hand of God. Some of the folks were a little afraid of that bouncing around; some of them slept, almost the whole way across. Somehow, I couldn't be either afraid or sleepily heedless of that sensation of being held in Your hand.

And when we landed . . . ! When I stepped down on British soil, I kept thinking of the Pilgrim Fathers who left this same soil, so many years ago, in a slightly different craft, for that fearful journey across the ocean to a land where they might worship God as they pleased. Roy laughed when I told him I was thinking of the Pilgrims; he said it was a strange thing to be thinking, in such a hubbub.

Hubbub is the word for it. Newsmen and cameramen crowded around us, shouting and laughing and interviewing and taking pictures. My first time through Customs was an experience—marked by the amazing courtesy and gentleness of the British Customs officials. Then we drove through the narrow, picturesque streets of London, past Buckingham Palace (where we saw the changing of the Guard, and what a spectacle *that* is!) and past wonderful Westminster Abbey.

I look down from my window at the quaint taxicabs in the streets, out across the Thames, and Big Ben is booming in the distance.

Let me not stumble among these people, Lord.
I am a stranger in a strange land—guide Thou my feet!

Thursday

A DAY of press interviews, and a three-hour reception. . . . Of course, there was the inevitable question, "What do you think of England?" I haven't been here twenty-four hours yet, and they asked me that! I gave what I thought then was the right answer: "I love London, and London's people . . . they are warm and friendly." Then I thought that might sound just a little phony, considering my short acquaintance with them.

But they *are* warm and friendly. I find most people everywhere to be warm and friendly; it's the oddity that is otherwise. And I love them for that.

I love Britain: first for what the people in Britain are, and second because their Pilgrims and Puritans brought the Christian faith from Britain to America, and established our nation on the Rock of Christ. That Rock was more important than Plymouth Rock!

One lady asked me about my "career." Was I satisfied with it, happy in it? I told her I thought my career might be worthwhile if it could be made to serve God. She looked startled. She gave me a half-cynical, searching look and asked, "Are you sincere?" Forgive me—I almost blew my top over that one. I replied, "Sincere, lady? Listen: my faith means more to me than the most brilliant career in the world. It's because of that faith that I came over here to help Billy Graham in his Crusade for Christ. If I were insincere, I'd be back home, making money." I hope she got it. I'd like to talk more with that gal. . . .

They asked Joan of Arc once if she thought she was "in a state of grace." She replied, "I think so; but if I am not, I pray the Lord to put me there, and quickly!" I feel the same way about grace—and sincerity.

Take from me all sham and pretense, Father;
if sincerity overwhelms me, then let me die.

Sunday

I HAVE never seen such beautiful churches as they have here. They take my breath. Great sweeping Gothic arches, massive buttresses and towers, ancient stained glass that sings hymns in color, carved stone and wood that shows forth the beauty of Thy handiwork!

But why are they so empty, so often only partially filled, if that? This morning I took Communion at eight o'clock in lovely old Carlisle Cathedral, the ancient "border" church, as we drove into Scotland. I couldn't believe my eyes: *there were only seven people at that service!* This is a *great* church. It is a 14th century dream. But—only seven people! It just doesn't make sense.

It isn't only here that the churches are empty; I have seen it and heard about it everywhere. I asked one fine friend in London why it was, and she gave me the strangest answer I have ever heard, to any question. "Well, you see," she said, "we British are a 'national crisis' people. We are at our best in a crisis. Then we get on our knees and ask God to help us. After it is all over, and everything is right again, we thank Him for His help, and then sort of go our own way again. Some folks have been trying to start a revival here, but I'm afraid it won't come off!"

Only in a crisis, Lord? What kind of religion is that? What must You think of us? (And by us, I mean not only the British, but *all* of us!) What must You think when we ignore You in all but the crises of life, and then come running to You like a lot of spiritual ne'er-do-wells, begging for a help we do not deserve?

My friend thinks the revival won't come off. It *must* come off. Maybe I sound now as though I were just praying in a crisis—but help us with this revival, God!

Give me a faith that is strong in the every-day give-and-take of life, O God, and not weakly frantic in time of peril!

Monday

THAT reply of my friend is still in my mind. This thought comes to me: somebody must have loved You a lot to build all those churches!

Make me aware of the few who love Thee, while I am surrounded by those who don't care.

Tuesday

HOW can I put down what was in my heart as those thousands of children cheered Roy in Glasgow? Some of them had been waiting since early morning, and it was two in the afternoon before we arrived. When I saw those little faces light up, as Roy came out to greet them, I couldn't hold back the tears.

If, somehow, they can see You in Roy, and realize that what they really love in him is Your spirit, maybe they will listen to him when he tells them to go to Sunday school and church.

Guess I'd better sign off now. Thank you for taking care of the folks at home.

May the beauty of Jesus be seen in us!

THERE is much stored up in me from this week in Glasgow. We had wonderful crowds every time we appeared.

Thank You for giving us courage to speak a word for You and Your servant, Billy Graham. The words evidently "clicked." The newspaper reviews have been both frank and kind, reacting sympathetically to the wholesomeness of our show. But they seemed so surprised that we should take time out in every show to honor You! They did say that our religion was "obviously genuine," so maybe I shouldn't wonder at their surprise.

Backstage, I sat almost despondent at the undercover opposition to our Christian effort. Then—thanks for sending him along, Lord!—a kindly little Christian minister walked over to me and thanked me so warmly for our "courage" in speaking a word for You in the show. He'll never know what he did for me, in that low moment. He'll never know how he cheered me and swept the uncertainty from my heart.

Why do we ever doubt, or fear? The Lord is on our side, and I will not fear what men may do to us. If He be for us, who can be against us?

You have given me fresh faith, God, and an incredible freedom to speak out.

They told us that when they scheduled the current Youth Rallies in Glasgow, they did not know that Roy and I would be here at the same time. They feel so definitely that You planned it that way, since we plug spiritual education and Sunday school attendance every time we appear. We should have known You would take care of it.

More and more, as the years pass, I feel that I plan none of my life, myself, but that every step I take is planned by You!

Saturday

SPENT a lovely day—first at Loch Lomond, and then in the Robert Burns country. Visited the cottage in which he was born, in Ayr. Saw the quaint fireplace in the cottage, the bed set in the wall, and stalls for the horses right in the house! Someone said something about "the good old days." If that was good, they can have it!

Yet, as I think of it now, I think You "fit the back to the burden." They "had it tough" in those days, and they said so; today, and 200 years hence, folks will think *they* "have it tough." It seems each generation has its peculiar trials. Who are we to say what the trials shall be?

I noticed on the records in Ayr that Mr. and Mrs.

Robert Burns lost two little girls in infancy. Maybe that was one reason why Burns is supposed to have had "the pulse of the common people," and that people came from near and far to listen to his magic poetry for a few minutes, just to get away from the daily grind. What a gift You gave him, Father: the gift of lifting people's spirits.

Apparently, "Bobbie" had his weaknesses, his doubts and despairs—but the gift You gave him lives on! He probably never knew just "how" he wrote that poetry; it just poured out of the reservoir You planted in his heart and mind.

How magnificent are Thy gifts to man, O God; how good it is that they are all so different! Make me search diligently to discover my talents—and help me to use them in Thy name.

Sunday

I SHALL never forget Saturday noon, at the hotel. Norman Roy, a shining-faced boy in a wheel chair, had lunch with us. Norman has been a fan of Roy's for years, and his great ambition was to "see Roy Rogers." He has a dread muscular disease, stricken at the age of 6. Now he's 16, and paralyzed from the waist down. He can barely raise his hands, but he can paint a little.

We learned from him that he has an older brother

who is also paralyzed! We talked with his mother, who said, "It's kind of hard . . . but where there's enough love, there's a way!"

How good it is for those of us who are healthy and strong that occasionally we can see in those less privileged a love that passes all understanding.

Monday

SPENT this morning at Mearnskirk Hospital. When we saw those long rows of little tiny girls lying encased in rigid braces, suffering from tuberculosis of the spine, —and when we heard their high little treble voices singing "Home on the Range," I almost cracked. Didn't dare look at Roy, because I knew he was about ready to "spill over," too.

We saw 300 little patients, and I saw the sun rise 300 times, as we approached their beds.

Oh, if we only had time to visit every such hospital in Britain!

It would be better for me to have a millstone hanged about my neck, than for me to neglect one sick or needy child that needs me.

Monday

DROVE through the Highlands today. What country! There were 7,000 people surrounding the hotel in Edinburgh when we arrived; we shook hands with as many as we could.

Roy took Trigger out of his van, and we went in and signed the hotel register—*all* of us, including Trigger.

Tomorrow we are going to Edinburgh Castle. Then Roy will go fishing for salmon (a day off!) and I am going to have lunch with Rev. Louis Evans Jr. (he's the son of our own beloved Dr. Louis Evans of Hollywood) and his wife, Colleen Townsend Evans.

Good night, Father. Thank You again for the blessings you have showered on us.

"The blessing of the Lord, it maketh rich. . . ."

Tuesday

THIS morning, I had the unforgettable experience of seeing Edinburgh Castle. Their beautiful shrine honoring You through their war dead is "out of this world."

I loved especially the stone carving representing a soul on its way heavenward, purified—or should I say sanctified—through human sacrifice bathed in the Blood of the Lamb.

Then we saw the room in which Mary Queen of Scots gave birth to James—he who "authorized" the King James Version of our Bible. In the tiny St. Margaret's Chapel, upstairs, I looked down at a copy of that Bible, open under glass, and I read the words, "The Lord is our refuge, and strength, a very present help in trouble." Poor ill-destined Mary probably read those words in this very place!

Also visited St. Giles Cathedral. The picture of the Ascension, in stained glass, is breath-taking. Somehow, the folds of Christ's white garment are brilliantly illuminated. I stood there thinking of how the disciples must have looked in awe at the illumination which constantly surrounded Christ.

The wood carving in the Chapel of the Knights of the Thistle was splendid, too; I loved that little carved angel with something resembling Scottish bagpipes!

Never let mine eyes become dull to Thy beauty, Lord; and let Thy Light shine forth in me, that those looking at me will see nothing but Light.

Tuesday (Evening)

THE lunch with the Evans family was wonderful! Louis has a small church here in Edinburgh . . . and he has an amazing understanding and depth for one so young. He said he was trying hard to "understand the other fellow's viewpoint and religious belief," so that he could meet that other fellow on his own ground and then carry him further to meet You in a vital, personal relationship. I believe he's right.

I think it takes understanding and sympathy to win people to You, more than it takes creed or dogma. It seems to be a too-common human failing in all of us to become impatient and even "righteously indignant" with people who disagree with us in matters of religion. We love to blast those who disagree with our particular brand of faith, and it's wrong. Jesus Himself had another method; we see it in His conversation with Nicodemus. He didn't blast Nicodemus; I think He loved that little questioner, though they differed widely. Jesus said, "Be ye wise as serpents and harmless as doves." I'm for that method.

I think of Will Rogers, too, who said once that he'd never met a man he didn't like. That's a good Christian statement.

I'm for young Louis Evans, and his approach. He'll win.

Help me as a Christian to keep my head and my temper, and to let the opposition lose theirs.

Wednesday

TONIGHT, as we left the hotel, there was quite a crowd in the street. A friend told me a good story about crowds. They were giving an uproarious welcome to the local football team in Glasgow, which was returning (with the bacon!) from a game in England.

An unobtrusive, quiet little man slipped unnoticed into the hotel. He really didn't amount to much, in such a crowd. He was only the man who discovered penicillin!

It set me thinking. I thought back to the day when I rode in a parade in San Diego, with several other Hollywood "celebrities," honoring a returning war hero. He was a real hero, quite worthy of honor; what bothered me was that the crowds poured out all their praise on the Hollywood celebrities, and seemed to forget the hero entirely! I thought of the countless obscure boys who had paid the last full measure of devotion, and here they were cheering us! It didn't seem right.

We have one tremendous satisfaction, Lord: while we may err in honoring men, and ignore those who deserve real honor, we know that the final accolade is in Your keeping. Only You can say, "Well done, good and faithful servant. . . ." Forgive us, and give honor where it is due.

Friday

GOT a new slant today. In a conversation with a theatre and a booking agency man; the theatre manager told me how much he liked the "Biblical" part of our show. We got to talking about the religious situation in England, and the agency man said, "The trouble with the church today is that it is no longer a church in the home." He seemed a little bitter about it; he had been a choir boy as a youngster, but somewhere along the line he drifted away. He also said that science had made things "so much easier" for us, and given us so much time free of work, that we had time on our hands in which to get into trouble. The result is that we are "vice-ridden." He explained that the rich had always been sinful because they had too much time in which to sin, while the serfs and peasants and workers spent all their time working, and subsequently were more "moral."

Maybe he's right, but I'm not too sure about it. Seems to me that the horns and the halos are distributed fairly evenly among the rich and the poor! But it does take us back to the old axiom that "an idle mind is the devil's workshop." He may have something there.

To me, the answer is not more work or more leisure: it is all-out commitment to You, be we rich or poor. The heart that opens to You will just not be interested in sin!

"Behold, I stand at the door and knock. If any man openeth, I will come in. . . ."

Monday

WE'RE in Birmingham. More crowds, singing "Home on the Range," in the streets.

We had the usual press conference. A lady traveling with us overheard one reporter say to another that he had come "to get a religious slant on Roy Rogers." He had his tongue in his cheek as he said that. Then he said, "I guess I'll have to change my plans, and my story. All these children singing out there in the street can't be all wrong about a man. I can't write what I planned."

I hope that spreads among the newsmen who have attacked Billy Graham before he has had a fair chance to state his case. They seem resentful that Billy has come "to draw Britain closer to God." May they change that story, God!

I read that "a little child shall lead them. . . ." Give us all, Father, the honesty and sincerity and buoyant faith of the children . . .

Tuesday

THE leaven is working sooner than I expected. Today there was a fine, fair article by a reporter who wrote of his opinion of Billy. The reporter is a brilliant writer and his newspaper is powerful. I may be wrong, but I think when Billy really goes to work, this premature attack on him will die in a hurry.

Tonight is his first service in Harringay Arena, Pack it, Lord!

And put coals of fire on Billy Graham's lips. . . .

Wednesday

WE DROVE today through a blinding snow-storm. Out in the country, we saw a lot of sheep lying placidly on the ground, while the snow almost buried them from sight. One of our party cried, "They will freeze to death!"

Oh, no! You have given them thick coats of wool as protection against that, and a natural animal warmth. They'll live.

You do the same for us, I think. The blasts are often so fierce that we become almost numb, but somehow You always manage to rekindle the flame at the crucial point, and we weather the storm.

May we put on the whole armor of God, and take unto ourselves the fire of Thy Spirit, to keep us through storm and strife.

Wednesday

WE'VE met a great soul in the person of Mr. Merrilees, Chief Constable of the Lothians. I think he is known better as a lay minister to the fatherless, the widows and the handicapped children of his district. A gem! I shall never forget riding with him over the countryside, in a driving rainstorm, and hearing him sing "The Lord's My Shepherd" as only a merry-hearted Scotsman could sing it!

He introduced us to little 13-year-old Marion, an orphan, who sang "The Cradle Song" for us. I had to turn my face away from her, so I looked at Roy. He stood there biting his lip, coughing, looking down at the floor and fingering his Stetson.

We want Marion to come over and visit us in America this year, during vacation. Will You help us work that out, Lord?

Mrs. Wilson runs the home for orphaned children,

in which we found Marion. She's one of the saintliest women I know. She has lost three of her own children. She tells me she went into her church and prayed, "Lord, You have taken my children, and I accept it. *But I cannot cure my loneliness. Please help me.*" How I know that feeling!

She says she heard God say, "Come! We will cure the loneliness. I have work for you to do." And He did—in that orphans' home.

That cured her loneliness.

> *Pure religion and undefiled before God and the Father is this, To visit the fatherless and widows in their affliction, and to keep himself unspotted from the world.*

Thursday

BAD news and good news today. The newspapers are criticizing us for putting that "Christian spot" in our show. One reviewer said he found it "embarrassing." Poor fellow, the shoe must have fit him too snugly. He said, "The Christian virtues of Roy's wife did nothing to help!" Well, if we have to accept that, help us to accept it for Your sake. And don't let us weaken in our witness.

They did speak a good word or two for Roy; they found him to be "No variety show artist . . . but unaffected, possessing a pleasing voice, simplicity, and much charm." The evening reviews were better; some were very nice.

We're grateful that no reporter, sympathetic or unsympathetic, has yet charged us with insincerity in our Christian effort. That is all-important.

And now for the good news! I went up the hill to pray in the great Cathedral. It was completely empty, except for one young man who was cleaning the place. Guess I was on my knees for 15 minutes; then I sat back in my chair and enjoyed the beautiful windows. The cleaning man came over and said, "Pardon me, lady, but may I tell you how wonderful it is to see you here, praying so fervently? Not many people drop in to pray here during weekdays, any more. There are only a few—but those few *really* pray!"

We sat and talked, for a long time. He told me about the Bishop of the Cathedral, who was tortured (both legs broken) by the Japanese in the late War. He also told me about himself, and of why he believed in prayer. Seems that he was scheduled to go into a hospital for a hernia operation; his wife was expecting a baby, and they had no money. He "didn't see how even the Lord could possibly pull me through all that," but he prayed anyway, and hard! He went into the hospital for the operation—but when they examined him they found that the hernia had completely disappeared! I suppose some would call that a "medical mystery," or something like that. I call it an answer to prayer.

The little cleaning man is grateful: "Now I can work, and use the money for our little baby's needs!"

He asked me about Billy Graham. What kind of

chap was Billy? I got in a good word there. He proudly showed me the great carved throne where the Bishop sat. I thought of Your word about the great serving the small.

A Bishop, and a cleaning man! It was a good day, Lord.

". . . and (he) took a towel, and girded himself. After that he poureth water into a bason, and began to wash the disciples' feet, and to wipe them with the towel. . . ."

Thursday (Later)

FATHER, two ladies are coming to give me some kind of award for "service to humanity," in *Angel Unaware*. Keep me humble, Lord.

They are officers of the National Association for Backward Children in Britain. How can I help them?

Let no one striving to do good come to me and go away without a piece of my heart.

Friday

HAD a busy day. Visited a great industrial plant, and talked with the proprietors, at lunch. They were curious as to what we were going to do with Billy Graham. They don't seem to understand this personal witnessing over here. That is, the average *layman* doesn't. They say "It's a bit too personal." There's something in them that shies away from the personal word spoken in public.

Why? Wasn't Jesus pretty personal, as He tried to reach persons? Wasn't He pretty "intimate" as He witnessed to the Glory of His Father? He was human, as well as divine. He admonished His disciples, "Go ye into all the world, baptizing them . . . and . . . *teaching*." And what does the gospel mean when it asks, "How shall they hear, except a preacher be sent?" That doesn't mean to keep quiet!

Should my neighbor be ill of a dread disease and I knew of a remedy that had cured me, I certainly would tell him about it. Well, I've got just that. You cured me. And I *will* tell about it, come what may!

Why are we so reticent to recommend the Greatest Physician of all? Is it that we are afraid of ridicule?

I confess it: sometimes I fear that ridicule. Give me courage back of my faith, Lord; one without the other is useless.

If we must be fools for Christ's sake, so be it; but let us never fear the ridicule of a fool.

Saturday

A NICE thing happened today. In the taxi on the way to our hotel, the driver turned around to us and said, "Pardon me for saying this, but I have to. You'll never know how Birmingham appreciates what you are doing for our children. I just thought you'd like to know how we all feel about it." Bless him!

We are ending our Birmingham engagement to-night. Roy and I took time out to visit two Occupational Centers for the Mentally Retarded, and a home for spastic children. I presented a combination radio and phonograph set to the children, given by their mothers.

Father, I seem to do fairly well when I'm talking to the children; it's the mothers that get me. When I see tears in their eyes, I seem to fall apart. I want to put my arms around every one of them and give them the comfort You gave me!

I wonder why the newspapers don't support these homes and projects for retarded children? They promised to send a photographer for this presentation, and they didn't. (The director of the Center wanted it to help in a fund-raising campaign.) The director said to me, "They don't want to give us any space in the papers at all." Great heavens, why? These people **don't** want to force their poor children on the public; all they want is a shelter for them, and a means of transportation to get them there.

It's awful to watch these children, in their difficulty boarding a bus; they are the targets of stares and ridicule! The newspapers make all sorts of excuses, when they are asked to help. It's what we call a "freeze-out," and it's despicable, and I resent it. (Watch that temper, Dale!) I was told by a newsman that perhaps one out of every eight mentally-handicapped children in Britain is a "Mongoloid"; if this statement is true, surely it should rouse concern on the part of the authorities."

> *Father, forgive them; they know not what they do . . . .*

Monday

THIS is Liverpool. I'll never forget Liverpool, for we were hardly here when both of us came down with the flu. We missed two performances. But we did have one funny thing happen.

Members of the Liverpool press visited us when we were up and around our rooms. So did Trigger—who walked up four flights of stairs, with a bunch of daffodils in his bridle, to cheer us up. He stood over Roy and shook the daffodils loose, out of his mane. I think he enjoyed it as much as we did!

We drove out, later, to the Heart Hospital for Children. And then to a home for retarded children, where we found some children, about 16 years old or 17, in bad shape. They couldn't sit up, and they moaned with pain. That hurt, Father. It hurt more to learn that many of the parents of these children never came near the place. How can they get like that?

How can people say, "Forget you ever had such a retarded child. Put him away, forget them, and go on leading a normal life!" How can a mother forget *any* child?

Saw one little "blue" baby boy at the Heart Hospital; the nurse came to me and said he wanted to give me a hug. I hugged him as hard as I dared, and hated to let go.

May I never walk selfishly in the light when I might be leading someone through the dark.

Tuesday

I'M GETTING impatient to be in London with the Billy Graham Crusade people. Today came word that approximately 3200 people have made decisions for You since Billy started his campaign. Also news that the churches in London are filling up, as a result of the campaign. Wonderful!

One newspaper article I read today said that Billy

is "utterly consecrated to God," and that it wasn't so much a matter of Billy being "a great theological preacher, as it is that he is so utterly sincere, and that he believes what he says about God." Good! It should be, must be that way. I don't believe that the mere wisdom of man can convert anybody; it takes a man completely sold on You to convert others.

And isn't it true that the greatest benefactors of men have been utterly humble and utterly sincere men —men who have had the grace to step aside and let You take over their minds and hearts?

Take my life, and let it be
Consecrated, Lord, to Thee.

Thursday

PLAYED in Belfast, Ireland, today. The auld sod! We put a shamrock in Trigger's bridle, and wore a bit o' the green ourselves. We're part Irish, You know. The audience responded well to our talk about Christianity and Billy Graham's Crusade—in spite of the fact that (we're told) there is real strife and intolerance between the churches here.

And we got to visit an occupational center for retarded boys, too. I find myself anxious to get through the show, when there's chance of making a visit like that. Had a lot of fun with those boys, and later with some tiny girls in Children's Hospital. I simply had to scoop up one little tot and run with him.

Is this a ministry You've led me to, God? If it is, I'm grateful, for there seems to be a great carelessness and neglect of these children. And if this is ministry, it's more fun than anything else my life has known!

Let me find them, and hold them in my arms, if only for a moment. And make them know that You love them even more than I do.

Saturday

Now it's Dublin. What a charming city! And what crowds! My heart nearly stopped when our taxi, coming from the station to the hotel, was surrounded by a surging, cheering mob. Some of the mothers holding little children were almost knocked off their feet. They lost their grasp on some of the children, and I thought sure they would be trampled and hurt. If just one child were hurt, I'm afraid I couldn't ever go on another tour.

When I announced tonight, in the show, that I would give every penny of royalty from the sale of *Angel Unaware,* on this tour, to the Association for Backward Children, the applause was thunderous. I'm sure they will help us, now.

A fine cleric came backstage tonight; he presented me with a prayer-book he had written for stage people, and asked me if it were true that we were going to help Billy Graham. He said, "Your Billy Graham is doing a fine work!" These Irish hearts are warm, Father.

Then a letter came from a sweet Irish couple who had just read *Angel Unaware,* and who on finishing it made a generous donation to the work of their Foreign Missionary Society. Robin will be remembered in many prayers said every year by the Society. It's hard to tell how deeply touched I was by that.

How insignificant do denominational lines become when we consider them in the light of Thy boundless love!

Tuesday

WE'RE here—in London! We had to get up at 6:45, to catch our plane—and it was the only plane not grounded at the airport on account of fog. Thank You!

Thank You too for stopping the rain at 2:30, just as our program got under way at Harringay Arena. Fifty thousand people came out to see us, and Trigger, and to hear our testimony. The people seemed so far away from the platform, but the message must have reached them, for Billy says there were approximately 900 decisions for You today,—and that many of them were *children!*

It was an "Arena," but the whole atmosphere of

the place was heavy with Your Presence. The 1,000-voice choir sounded like an angelic host. We were almost overcome as people came pouring down those aisles to give themselves to You—and I forgot to bring a handkerchief!

They represented every church, every denomination, every walk of life. Some of them, frankly, were only curious; some were a little doubtful, some were sincerely seeking Your truth, and some were beautifully confident of Your salvation. But all were attentive. When we spoke, the silence was deafening. There was no applause, for which I was grateful.

Just make them listen, Lord; give them ears to hear, and hearts to understand.

Thursday

A GREAT day for You, and for us. We visited 600 patients at Fountain Hospital for Backward Children. A number of them are Mongoloids. One little blonde, brown-eyed three-year-old seemed fascinated by my Stetson hat. He looked like little Robin's twin! He smiled, and held out his arms to me; I found it almost impossible to leave him.

Billy preached a powerful sermon last night. At the end of it people literally swarmed into the prayer rooms. Billy was feeling quite ill when the meeting started, and we were all praying for him. Halfway through his sermon he turned around to us and whispered, "Boy, I feel great!"

He's certainly *going* great: in the meeting tonight we saw 533 people come down the aisles to give You their lives.

Guide him, God. We're winning!

Saturday

LAST night, Billy told us that the attendance for this first month of the Crusade was around 450,000. About 8,500 decisions have been won. The "underground" (subway) is jammed for every meeting; they put up signs now, "Harringay Overcrowded" to discourage any more from coming! Nothing like it has happened to London in a long, long time.

> *"Multitudes, multitudes in the valley of decision: for the day of the Lord is near in the valley of decision."*

Sunday

WE SPOKE at Billy's meeting at Harringay—and got, from one man, the strangest welcome ever! When Roy and I had finished speaking, Billy stepped up to the pulpit and said, "Roy Rogers and Dale Evans are not seeking publicity when they talk like that about Jesus Christ!" at which a loud, rowdy voice roared up from somewhere in the audience, "How is it they sing the songs they did in the Stadium last Saturday, and then come in here and sing about Jesus?" Billy, wisely, ignored it.

We don't mind a little honest heckling, Father—and these folks over here are good hecklers! But this one was below the belt. What songs was he objecting to? Roy sings one called "Skyball Paint" (a yodelling comedy song about a rodeo horse) and "A Four Legged Friend" (a funny song about Trigger from the picture "Son of Paleface.") I have a song, "Don't Ever Fall in Love With a Cowboy," and another, the popular "Over the Rainbow," into which we have written some Christian lyrics. Father, these are *clean* songs; we have never sung anything but clean songs. Is the fact that there is a little humor injected here supposed to be sinful?

We discussed the songs we would sing, coming down on the plane from Dublin, and we decided it was best to let the children see us first as they expected, with Trigger, and then to "level" with them with our Christian testimony. These children had never seen us, or Trigger, in person, and we thought it best to do it that way. But then we went right into two more songs—"Lord, Keep Your Mighty Hand on Me," and "Christian Cowboy," and Roy closed with a plea for the youngsters to go to church and Sunday school every Sunday. They tell us that a huge crowd of those boys and girls went directly from that meeting to Harringay Arena, to hear Billy Graham, and that many of them gave their hearts to Christ. Is that bad?

Singing Western songs is part of our job; it seemed wisest to us to entertain the children first, particularly the small ones, before speaking to them about You. Wasn't it Paul who said that he became "all things to all men" in order to win a few to You? Was he wrong, too?

A reporter asked Roy if an actor in show business could "really" be a Christian! Roy answered, "Certainly! I know lots of good Christians in Hollywood. Acting is just a job, so far as I am concerned. But all some of you reporters seem to want to write about Hollywood people are the bad things. There are a lot of good things happening, too, but you never print that! Guess some people would rather read the bad things!" It's true.

People's hearts have to change; then the newspapers will change.

"What is man, that thou are mindful of him?... Thou hast made him a little lower than the angels. . . ."
Doesn't that go for all men, Lord?

STILL thinking about that reporter's question, and Hollywood people. I suppose this reporter is impressed by the fact that there are so many divorces among us in Hollywood, and among stage people in general. There are. It isn't right. But that divorce rate is high in other places, too! We all regret these short Hollywood marriages—but I know of scores of "unsung" marriages out there that are of fifteen, twenty, twenty-five years duration, and still going strong! But successful marriages never make the headlines; it's the "changing partners" that are eligible as "news."

I think we need to take a *prayerful* attitude toward this, and not a critical one. If we would all pray for each other more, maybe a lot of these "changing partners" might be changed. I'm sure that if these folks in the lurid headlines knew You in a more vital way, things would be different.

I believe, with all my heart, that this frequent changing of mates is really caused by a deep sense of insecurity. I believe these people are chasing rainbows, looking for an earthly paradise that just isn't there. What they really seek is peace of mind and soul—and they haven't yet realized that such peace is found only in You, and not in anything or anyone human. If they only knew You and Your perfect love and peace, they would learn to love each other more and to overlook a lot of their silly, petty grievances, and they would know that no one of us is perfect!

Every one of us has his particular faults. You alone, Lord, are perfect, and completely satisfying to a hungry human soul.

Save me from hypocrisy, Lord: may I be Christian enough to cast the beam out of my own eye before I go after the mote in my brother's.

Tuesday

BILLY preached a thriller on "Repentance" tonight. It was one of the finest sermons I've ever heard. But at the end of it a man shouted out of the crowd, "Mr. Graham, why don't you pray for your President Eisenhower to stop this cold war?" Billy never even looked toward the man; he bowed his head for a moment, and then he said, "It's time we stopped looking to man. Let us turn our eyes toward God!"

Thank You for that divinely inspired answer.

Our help is in the name of the Lord, who made heaven and earth.

Wednesday

I HAVE seen many wonderful places in England. Today we were in Windsor Castle, with its beautiful St. George's Chapel. There is a statue here of the Princess Charlotte, who died in childbirth, and it is glorious. The other marble figures of the Royal Tombs are remarkably life-like, especially those of Queen Mary and King George. The guide told us that Queen Mary posed for the "lying in state" effigy several times, during her life. At first it seemed a bit morbid; but then—why not? Such thought for the end of life might make us all a little more careful about the middle of life! And in the midst of life we are in death!

More alive than all this is the thought that all the fine old churches I've been seeing in and about London have stood steadfast through such danger and peril, all down the long centuries. St. Paul's is lovely—especially that high dome that stood so firm through the bombings of the last war. I shall always remember quaint old St. Bartholomew's; Londoners say that this gallant old place is "haunted," and that on occasion "the ghostly outline of a monk" can be seen at night, but I am more interested in the way these old churches have been preserved through centuries of war, persecution, fire and plague. There they stand, mutely witnessing!

Give me a church in my heart like this, Lord: a church to stand so firm that the gates of hell cannot prevail against it.

Thursday

SPEAKING of fire and war and bombings, Jack Thomas of the *Empire News* told me an incredibly beautiful story today. He said that he was sent, during a bombing raid in the last War, to try to persuade one mother to get down into a bomb shelter before she and her children were blown to bits. All around her house were other houses, either completely destroyed or in flames. He walked into her house to find her seated in the middle of her living room, reading the Bible to her two children. Jack pleaded with her to leave the house. She looked up at him, smiling serenely, and said, "We are perfectly safe. You see, Jesus Christ is here with us." And she turned back to read from her Scriptures. . . .

Her house still stands. Jack says, "Every time I pass it, I think of that scene. I shall never forget the faith of that woman."

Oh Thou who art the calm heart of all things, give me a faith that will keep me as calm as that!

THE Queen Mother, Elizabeth, has written a beautiful appeal to the mothers of her Realm to take a stand for Christianity and to lead their children to You. Bless her royal heart!

Church today in the Queen's Chapel at the Savoy. Later we met Mr. and Mrs. Arthur Rank—he has produced two fine Christian films—"The Promise," dealing with Jesus' promise of a Comforter, and "Which Will Ye Have?", the story of Pilate's release of Barabbas. The final scene in this picture of Barabbas I will never forget; Barabbas walks to the foot of the cross, smiting his breast, with torment on his face, crying, "He took my place. He died for me. I shall have to live for Him!"

The producer, Mr. Rank, is as amazing as his picture. He told us that he felt the picture should never be shown without having someone extending an invitation to accept Christ, before it starts.

And "picture people" are supposed to be bad!

Dear God, stop every man, now and then, dead in his tracks, and ask him, "Do you really understand that He died for you?"

Monday

OUR last night at the Billy Graham meetings. How I hate to leave! But we are leaving on a wondrous note.

Somehow, I felt led to tell of the miracle of Your guiding hand that had come to us in the adoption of Dodie and Sandy. I don't know why, but I just had to tell about it, as my part in the early part of the meeting at Harringay Arena. My heart told me I must, but I was embarrassed and felt I could not ask Billy for extra time to tell the whole story. I was startled when he walked into the waiting room and said, "Dale, you and Roy take all the time you want tonight!" So I did. I just let You tell the whole story. . . .

Then Billy took over, and said to his crowd, "I did not know what Dale was going to talk about, and she certainly did not know the content of my sermon—but tonight I am speaking on *Adoption!*" He went on to explain how much more wonderful is our adoption into the Kingdom of God. Most humans want the smartest, prettiest and healthiest baby they can find, to adopt; but You don't care how ugly *we* are, or how unhealthy our souls. You never turn any of us down, if we ask You to take us in.

One of the top actresses of England—how beautiful she was!—was adopted into the Kingdom tonight. She fairly ran down the aisle to the prayer-room.

And side by side with her were the lame, the halt, the ugly, the blind—all stepping out together on the new sunlit road to glory, in company with Your Son. . . .

". . . He died for all, that they which live should not henceforth live unto themselves, but unto him which died for them, and rose again."

Thursday

HOME again, in California! How good this California sun feels! Had a little sinus trouble during our last days in London but it's gone in two days flat, in this sun.

And the family!—I couldn't hold back the tears as we all rushed together after this long separation. Coming home is so good for the soul.

But working with Billy Graham was good for our souls, too! Just as we left, Jack Thomas (he of the *Empire News*) said to us, "I have attended meetings before—but never meetings like these! What impressed most was the look on the faces of the people who came forward when Billy gave his invitation. I'd normally expect people, when they take a step like that, to have a 'cowed' look. But no—these folks had a look of indescribable triumph and victory. I've never seen anything quite like it."

And we were told at the start that the revival couldn't possibly come off among this "national crisis" people!

Forgive us, God, for not expecting big things of You . . . and for not helping to bring them off!

Friday

IT'S quiet now. The furore of home-coming has died down a little, and I think this might be a good time for me to sort of check up and evaluate my faith. I have seen such marvelous things happening in the field of faith these past few weeks, that I want to be sure of my own!

People are forever asking me what I believe. Here it is:

I believe in the Bible. With it, my soul is fed, and I wonder how my soul could be fed at all without it. I get all kinds of books and periodicals from kind friends all over the world, and I enjoy them. But I know they will understand when I say I enjoy Your Word most of all. This Bible, to me, has "top priority" in my life. I think it is a Book which you either believe, or you don't believe. I believe it, and in it, and my life has been made unbelievably rich because of that belief, and that one Book.

I believe in the Christ of the Book; perhaps I err in putting belief in the Bible first, for actually it is the Christ of the Book in which I base my whole faith. He changed my life. I'm not interested in arguing about that; it's a fact. With Christ, too, you either accept or deny. There isn't any middle ground about Him. Either you believe in Him, or you don't. Either He was the Christ, the Son of God, the Only Begotten, the Lamb, the Light, or He wasn't. I believe in Jesus Christ as the Saviour of the world. I believe He is the Messiah. I believe You so loved the world that You gave Your Only Begotten Son, that whosoever believeth in Him should not perish, but have everlasting life.

I believe in You, in God, as the Father of our Lord Jesus Christ and as the Creator of all that lives and moves and has its being. I believe You are the kindly heart at the centre of the universe; I believe that all things move at Your command. I believe You made both meteors and men for a purpose, and I want to spend my life in discovering and helping that purpose.

If someone asks me to prove all this, scientifically, I can only say this: I believed that You and Your Son would give me a new life in place of an old, unhappy one—and You did. I want no proof about that. Nor am I interested in debating it.

It happened to me, so I *know* in whom I have believed.

I believe it shall never end for me: I believe in immortality and eternal life. I believe my soul will ultimately be with You, and that I shall find a new, glorified body in eternity.

This I believe. And I am serenely confident that You will lead me into green pastures, as my Shepherd, and that goodness and mercy shall follow me all the days of my life, and that I shall dwell in the house of the Lord forever.

Oh, there is more, Lord; there are other details in my faith. But these are the peaks, the mountains.

This I believe, O God; if I err, put me right; if it is good, strengthen it. If there come any unbelief, transform it into faith.

Saturday

SOMETHING wonderful happened this morning: I was told that Children's Hospital, here in Los Angeles, is to have a special clinic for mentally retarded children! The good doctor who was with Robin at the end called Art Rush and asked him if we would like to help on the project. We will, to the best of our ability.

Wouldn't it be wonderful if doctors or nurses could use a new technique when they have to tell a parent that their baby is defective—if they could only say, "You are the parents of an angel in disguise, and if you will accept this child as a spiritual blessing, your lives will be enriched beyond measure!"

What a great truth You taught us, Father, when You told us to "Cast thy bread upon the waters, (and) thou shalt find it after many days." Robin cast her spirit upon us, and it has come back in a clinic!

Thursday

A LETTER from Jack Thomas, in London. . . . He says Billy Graham's campaign is "going from strength to strength." The secular press in England is bewildered . . . trying to find superlatives to describe it . . . can't believe what they are seeing. . . . A meeting in Hyde Park drew 75,000 people. . . . The atheists have had their soapboxes in Hyde Park for years, but I wonder if their *accumulative* audiences, over all that time, would amount to anything like 75,000! . . . They turn out in a pouring rain at Harringay and Wembley Stadium, and sit through the rain to hear Billy. . . . Wembley authorities say they marveled at a crowd of 100,000 for a national football final, but they had 120,000 for Billy, and they could only say that it was "a fabulous, almost unbelievable spectacle." . . . They come even from Wales and Scotland. . . . One paper says, "No preacher in history has ever faced an audience as large as Billy Graham had at Wembley." It could be so. . . .

They come because they're hungry, Lord: feed these sheep—now, with Billy, and after Billy is gone.

Sunday

WHILE speaking at a church in Colton, Cal., recently, the pastor asked *me* to take up the offering; I did, on condition that he let me send the money to help the American Indians. It goes to help a Mississippi Indian boy through a Christian school.

That was for Dodie. Roy is calling her "a prize package" now. I am hoping that we can wrap up a few prize packages for her Indian people. That's the least we can do, in thankfulness for her.

The command is to "preach the gospel to every creature." God, let me never think of it on a smaller scale than that. May my horizons never be fixed, but constantly pushing back.

Monday

SAT in my car this morning at a filling-station, and tuned in on Dr. Jack MacArthur preaching; it was glorious. We like Dr. Jack; Roy, Cheryl and I came into the church through his ministry.

I remember how we used to get all excited, Dr. Jack and I, as we "argued" about the person and work of Jesus Christ. I thought he was a bit old-fashioned, maybe even a little intolerant, in those days, for then I had a tendency to minimize the cross and to play up "the divinity of man." It is not so now. Now I understand that man simply cannot save himself, and that he must accept the free gift of eternal life through the sacrifice of Jesus on His cross. It just can't come any other way. Paul was right when he said that we should "work out your own salvation with fear and trembling;" he meant, didn't he, that it must be worked out through Christ? I believe that "there is none righteous, no not one." If it were possible for us to attain perfection for ourselves, then the crucifixion of our Lord would be of no value, and He would be a laughing-stock, indeed!

I suppose some will call me "old-fashioned" in this belief, but my experience tells me otherwise. I hunted, and hard, for inner peace and certainty, with the old-fashioned "I-am-perfect" method, and got nowhere; I never found it until I threw myself at the foot of the cross in complete self-surrender.

The old pharisaical "I-am-perfect" brand of peace was as fickle as the wind; it came and went and it always left me struggling like a spent swimmer in the water. Your peace stayed with me. It has braced me in the toughest storms and trials—and if that isn't the final test of peace, what is?

Dr. Jack put it well this morning when he said, "Jesus Christ is no security *against* storms, but He *is* security in the midst of them." Our blessed Lord said, "In the world, ye shall have tribulation, but be of good cheer; I have overcome the world." Thus, we, through

Him, also can overcome the storms. I believe that, for I have seen it work in my life.

Keep my house of faith rooted in the rock of Christ, O God, and I shall never again fear storm or strife or any other testing of my soul.

Tuesday

WE MET today to plan a Christian film with a western background. It was the most exciting meeting our staff has ever had.

If You want us to do this, Father, it will be one celluloid task that I shall thoroughly enjoy. We'll do it if You want it. Let us know.

"For thou art my rock and my fortress; therefore for thy name's sake lead me, and guide me."

One Month Later

THOU knowest my down-sittings and uprisings! And I have certainly had to sit down for the past month. I've been in the hospital with an inner ear infection, and now I'm home recuperating, and trying to make myself believe it all happened to me.

It started at night. In bed, my ear started to roar in a frightening way. I lay there pondering the dream I had, some months back—remember?—when the angel put her fingers to my lips and said, "Be still!" The dream came back in the roaring; somehow, it all seemed connected.

Soon after this, we had Redd Harper and his family for dinner. (Redd had asked permission to record my little song, "Happy Birthday, Gentle Saviour," for a Christmas release.) We were discussing our British experiences when suddenly the roaring came again, and the table began to dance around. I had to clutch the table to keep from falling. I recovered enough to sit at the piano awhile and work with Redd on the song. Thank You, Father, for letting me do that before "the boom was lowered."

Thinking I was only over-tired, I took a sedative. The next morning I couldn't get out of bed; I staggered to my feet, had a violent nausea, and toppled back on the bed.

The doctor came, took one look at me, and took me to the hospital for endless tests. After three days of constant nausea, I was even too ill to pray. But You took care of that. This happened to be a hospital in which prayers were said morning and evening through a loud-speaker in the halls. Even those of us too ill to pray could listen and open their hearts to You!

I had a chance to help one of the sick—a little girl who was undergoing dangerous surgery. I wrote her a long letter—and she sent back the sweetest note, saying that the letter had helped her, and that she wasn't afraid. We do get chances to help, even in the depths of our own pain.

They sent me home on the eighth day. I couldn't watch the traffic without becoming dizzy, so I kept my eyes glued on the clock on the dashboard all the way back to Encino. My Mom is here with me now. She is one of those deep-down Christians who enjoy "doing for others."—She isn't happy unless she is "doing."

I'll be all right, Lord. Thank You for going to the hospital with me, and for staying there through my pain.

"If I ascend up into heaven, thou art there: if I make my bed in hell, behold thou art there."

Thursday

THE dizziness and faulty equilibrium are slowly leaving me; slowly, but it's going. I want to thank You now for this experience. Particularly, for the *warning*. You had to do it this way, to make me understand that I had to slow down, and that I just couldn't keep up the pace I have been traveling for the past year or so. I know now that I haven't any right to complain about the illness, any more than a backslider has any right to kick about the sound of a church bell calling him to worship! You were ringing a bell of warning with this siege of labyrinthitis, and I'm grateful that I heard it, and understood it.

Now I'll slow down, and so be able to serve You longer.

> *This sickness is not unto death, but for the glory of God, that the Son of God might be glorified thereby.*

THE other day a call came for Roy, from a boy who was on his way Home. He had one last request: he wanted to see Roy Rogers. They said they would bring him in an ambulance, to see Roy at the house. I had to be at the doctor's office, so I couldn't see him, much as I wanted to.

Roy told me later that "I wouldn't have missed seeing that little guy for anything in the world." They had a great time together.

Then Roy got a wire saying that the little fellow had gone on, with a great big smile on his face because he had seen Roy!

Both Roy and I appreciate the tremendous responsibility we have in situations like this—and there are many such situations. Keep us humble, God, and ready to do what You want us to do. Give us strength, give us patience, give us understanding. Teach us!

It will go on and on and on, I think, so long as there are people, and so long as people need You. There will always be pleasure, there will always be pain; there will always be work for the Christian to do, in both pleasure and pain.

Help us to help; that's all we live for, now. Let no dawn catch us unprepared; let no sunset overtake us without some word spoken for You, some wanderer guided back on the home-road, some soul made thankful and wanting to sing.

May we take no thought for the morrow, except to do that and be like that on the morrow, and beyond that, make us to be still, and to know that You are God!